TEACHING VULNERABLE LEARNERS

TEACHING VULNERABLE LEARNERS

Strategies for Students Who Are Bored, Distracted, Discouraged, or Likely to Drop Out

SUZY PEPPER ROLLINS

W. W. Norton & Company

Independent Publishers Since 1923

This work is intended as a general information resource for teachers and school administrators. Although the author has extensive experience in the subject matter, neither the author nor the publisher can guarantee that any educational approach, strategy or technique that this book describes or proposes will work with every individual student. The author is not a lawyer, and nothing contained in this book should be construed as legal advice.

Any URLs displayed in this book link or refer to websites that existed as of press time. The publisher is not responsible for, and should not be deemed to endorse or recommend, any website other than its own or any content, including any app, that it did not create. The author, also, is not responsible for any third-party material.

For information about permission to reproduce selections from this book, write to
Permissions, W. W. Norton & Company, Inc., 500 Fifth Avenue, New York, NY 10110

For information about special discounts for bulk purchases, please contact
W. W. Norton Special Sales at specialsales@wwnorton.com or 800-233-4830

Manufacturing by Versa Press
Production manager: Katelyn MacKenzie

Library of Congress Cataloging-in-Publication Data

Names: Rollins, Suzy Pepper, author.
Title: Teaching vulnerable learners : strategies for students who are bored, distracted,
discouraged, or likely to drop out / Suzy Pepper Rollins.
Description: First edition. | New York : W.W. Norton & Company, [2020] |
Series: Norton books in education | Includes bibliographical references and index.
Identifiers: LCCN 2019052136 | ISBN 9780393714623 (paperback) | ISBN 9780393714630 (epub)
Subjects: LCSH: Students with social disabilities—United States. |
Students with disabilities—United States. | Academic
achievement—United States. | Teacher-student relationships—United States.
Classification: LCC LC4091 .R65 2020 | DDC 371.826/94—dc23
LC record available at https://lccn.loc.gov/2019052136

W. W. Norton & Company, Inc., 500 Fifth Avenue, New York, N.Y. 10110
www.wwnorton.com

W. W. Norton & Company Ltd., 15 Carlisle Street, London W1D 3BS

2 3 4 5 6 7 8 9 0

For my teachers at North Shore High School
in Houston, Texas, especially:

Jean Rose, for teaching me how to think
Jackie Gilbreath, who forced me to be on the debate team
Maisie Temme, who gave me a sense of belonging

Nothing can ever repay you for the dedication and commitment
you showed to me and every other student who
walked in that building each and every day.
Know that it mattered . . . and worked.

Contents

Introduction

I n peril, in jeopardy, at risk. These are all synonyms for the word *vulnerable*, which derives from a Latin word meaning "to wound." One can rightfully argue that all students are academically vulnerable at different points in their schooling. The groups discussed here, however, include large numbers of learners who are not reaching their potential in our classrooms. In fact, some are doing heartbreakingly poorly. When we see them in the hallways or in class, they might not appear vulnerable at all; in fact, some might be accumulating suspensions—or absences. Or they might not say much at all. But if they continue on this troubling academic path, they may indeed become wounded, in terms of job opportunities, mental and physical health, and the shape of their lives going forward.

This book is also about the awe-inspiring impact that educators have on students. The power of what teachers and leaders do in buildings can literally change the entire trajectory of these students' lives. The way that we teach, the connections we forge, and even the students we deliberately include in extracurricular activities have the amazing power to transform imperiled students to successful adults.

When I was constructing my second book for the Association for Supervision and Curriculum Development, *Teaching in the Fast Lane*, one paragraph in a research journal was so jolting that I tucked it away for later study. It was about the staggering percentage of students with ADHD who wind up incarcerated. I thought, "How could I not know this?" This largely genetic disorder that afflicts boys more often than girls is the focus of Chapter 1. This group of children, numbering in the millions, is in real jeopardy. Academically, their innate struggles with distractibility and limited attention make schoolwork a real challenge for students with ADHD.

Low grades, reduced likelihood of college entry, and underemployment are just the surface of their potential problems. Sadly, they often perceive that educators don't even care about them. Particularly disconcerting is their higher propensity to suffer from emotional issues, substance abuse, and even suicide than their peers. Getting these learners on the right path academically and socially can literally change lives. Without help, they are more likely to be incarcerated not just once, but multiple times. But with targeted help, the outcomes can be quite different. There is another side to ADHD; some of the most successful entrepreneurs in the world not only have the disorder, they view it as a gift. They contend that some of the same traits that make school so challenging are just right for the business world, like creativity and risk taking. In fact, the same students who struggle to sit still in a desk often become business owners, entertainers, and athletes. Their futures largely depend on what educators and families do to help them thrive—not just survive—in school.

In Chapter 2, I look at the fastest-growing group of students in the United States, now around 10% of our learners: students classified as English language learners (ELLs). It's hard to fathom what their school days are like as they take notes on a lesson about chemical reactions, read a Walt Whitman poem, and try to figure out what a parabola is—all in a language they barely understand. These learners are largely situated in general education content classrooms, and teachers are tasked with supporting students' language acquisition while teaching science or social studies. As a whole, this group is not reaching their academic potential, with a startlingly low graduation rate and much lower college entrance rates than their English-proficient peers. Schools are grappling with the best balance of learning English alongside content. The good news is that there are effective teaching principles that every educator can implement today to more effectively support their learning. Even better news: the same basic instructional strategies will likely enhance the progress of the native English-speaking students in class as well.

Chapter 3 is about reading, the cornerstone of every child's academic success. Not only the toughest chapter to construct, this may be the most difficult to digest. The stark news here is that there are large gaps in reading readiness as students enter our kindergarten and first grade classrooms. Children whose parents or caregivers have read to them every day may walk into our doors a full year ahead. What happens before children ever begin school, in vocabulary development and reading readiness, is so critical to their academic careers that it warrants community efforts to generate change. What happens after we meet them is the next stage in their literacy development, which should include science-based reading strategies that will advance every reader. But it's not just a job for the early elementary years, although those teachers certainly do a lot of the heavy lifting. Every content subject involves navigating text. To create college-ready readers (and move stagnant reading scores) requires, in my view, a pre-K through 12th grade plan to build readers.

Not being a proficient reader can take a lifelong toll. Students who are not good at reading tend to be sick more often and have more behavioral issues; some simply withdraw from class activities. As adults, weak readers are much more likely to be on welfare and make lower wages. In a pattern that is often perpetuated, children of parents with low literacy levels tend to have similar weak reading levels. Creating good readers can interrupt the pattern, changing students' lives and enriching communities by increasing educational attainment and job opportunities, and even breaking the poverty cycle. There's an old urban myth that prison officials plan cell space by third grade reading scores. That's not true—but it could be, because a high percentage of inmates are largely illiterate.

The focus of Chapter 4 may seem like a mismatch for a book about vulnerable learners: gifted students. Often, these learners have quite unique qualities that require different instructional thinking. For example, their intellectual gifts may outpace their physical development, and their interests and conversational levels may be more aligned with those of their teachers than of their peers. Some of these students may enter the classroom already knowing most of what is going to be taught. As general education teachers dig deep to move other students to proficiency through additional practice and review, gifted students often await moments for intellectual challenges. There are solutions to support these learners in reaching their potential. And some don't cost a dime.

Chapter 5 concerns a diverse set of students that cuts across many different populations but merges together by middle or high school into one highly vulnerable group: students at risk of dropping out of school. And while the dropout forms are completed in high school, many factors along the way contribute to the growth of this group. As counterintuitive as this may sound, grade-level retention is a practice that exacerbates dropout. Implemented with good intentions, this policy often applies to third graders who fail to pass their state reading tests. This "get tough on reading" approach, research indicates, may inadvertently create more dropouts while failing to show lasting progress on reading.

Retention is but one factor in dropout. At one time in our history, students left school to get married or join the military. The trend over time has changed. Today, more students leave due to failing grades and a general dislike of school. The good news is that schools are developing innovative solutions. Reduced reliance on canned computer packages has been a positive trend, because we know that struggling students don't progress well on those. (High-achieving students do!) Rather, more hands-on, real-world lessons with supportive teachers work. And acceleration can yield positive results. In this approach, students are provided just enough prior knowledge, academic vocabulary, and scaffolding in time for new learning so that they latch on to concepts, rather than requiring them to backtrack and relearn skills in the context of old lessons. Acceleration tactically supports vulnerable learners so they can learn on pace with their peers, instead of being perpetually behind.

Failing students can confound the most passionate educators. Through our lens, the solutions seem easy: work harder, pay attention, do your homework. Chapter 6 is about why they often don't. The basics of motivation are explained here, as are the reasons why, on some days, students seem to barely move. Some of these students have traumatic experiences in their backgrounds. Because while the umbrella topic of this chapter is crafting motivational lessons that can move students to work, lessons occur within a classroom and larger school environment. These particularly vulnerable students may respond unexpectedly to benign happenings in class, and understanding some of the signs of trauma is helpful to supporting these learners. Other demotivated students may have experienced the repercussions of a contentious educational trend: zero tolerance discipline policies. What began as school safety initiatives somehow widened into suspensions for minor infractions. And while there are students who need to be suspended for safety reasons, every day they miss content in class, they get further behind.

Students are often in more than one group. For example, a gifted student might have ADHD traits, in the same way that a low-performing reader might. And when we talk about students in danger of dropping out, all groups merge. It may surprise some that gifted students drop out as well.

COMMON THEMES

Researching these topics, it became vibrantly clear to me why outstanding teachers produce positive academic results for just about every student in their classrooms. Certain effective instructional practices clearly stood out across the research, regardless of the population.

- For all students, **connecting to prior knowledge** is hugely important. We learn better, we read better, and we listen better when we can connect new information to what we already know.
- **Scaffolding** is important for every group, except perhaps gifted students. We cannot expect students to remember everything they have been taught. But the scaffolding looks different for varying groups. ELL students benefit from language scaffolding, ADHD students from memory and organizational scaffolding, and at-risk learners in general often need scaffolding for prerequisite skills.
- **High-interest, valuable tasks** matter for every group of learners and is a cornerstone of student motivation.
- Ongoing **vocabulary development** with multiple exposures over time in varying ways supports learning across the board. All day long, teachers use new academic vocabulary. Students need time to draw, play games, and have conversations with the words.
- Several chapters discuss the **use of stations** as an instructional design. In stations, students become involved in learning a concept through tactical, diverse ways. After engaging in a vocabulary sort and quick write at station one, for example, they physically move to station two to examine primary sources. Stations are thoughtful, purposeful, flexible groups that move. This approach allows for easy differentiation for different learners. For English learners, there might be a video aspect or text with more visuals. For gifted learners, advanced readings might be included. And while stations are not utilized every day, this model

allows teachers time to address individual needs of students, which is difficult to do in whole-group settings.

For the expert teacher, many of these strategies will resonate as techniques that are already in use in their classrooms. For vulnerable groups of students, however, these strategies must be consistently present. Our children in academic trouble require high-impact instruction to catch up, get back in the game, and move on.

A big surprise for me was the impact of extracurricular activities. For every single group discussed in the book, experts from separate fields strongly recommended encouraging students' outside interests. Playing sports or being involved in a club provides avenues for developing students' strengths beyond academics. They develop relationships with other students and adults and find a place of belonging. Inclusive policies for sports and clubs are encouraged to strengthen students' participation and engagement.

This book will not provide every answer. Rather, the hope is that conversations will be sparked about innovative ways to help underperforming students reach their potential. And while this is largely about academic vulnerability, it's clear that how children do in school has a tremendous and lasting impact on their lives—their physical and mental well-being, the colleges they enter, the jobs they secure, the income they will receive. Unfortunately, even incarceration is directly connected to academic progress.

Students in academic dark holes may not look vulnerable at all. In fact, they might frequently have their heads on their desks, arrive every day without writing utensils, or appear ready to pick a fight with anyone in range. These students may not seem to be in jeopardy, but they certainly are. They are, in fact, quite breakable.

TEACHING VULNERABLE LEARNERS

CHAPTER 1

Explorers in Desks

J etBlue is a different kind of airline. From ice cream pints for travelers to accepting selfies as boarding passes, JetBlue has made a unique mark on the airline industry. Its founder, David Neeleman, has unique qualities as well. He has ADHD, but rather than viewing it as a curse, he largely considers the diagnosis a gift. In fact, he has shared his view that some of the traits of ADHD have actually provided him with distinct advantages over others in the business arena (Shankman, 2017).

Neeleman didn't win any awards for academics. He did so poorly on the ACTs that a school counselor informed him that he would have scored higher if he'd just marked all the C answers instead of trying at all. When asked how he could explain the connection between being an entrepreneur and having ADHD, he theorized that students who do very well in school, for example, make straight As and get on a college track, typically get a job, and stay in that lane. Students with ADHD, however, often don't get on a track. He even jokes that these kids are often "thrown out of a boat." Therefore, they often create their own solutions and forge their own tracks (Shankman, 2017).

Interestingly, Neeleman wasn't officially diagnosed with ADHD until adulthood. The diagnosis was a relief. He finally understood some of his behaviors. He'd always felt like he had just bluffed his way through school and was not smart. Now, he got it. It would be easy for him not to share his story—in fact, some advised against it—but he believes that kids with ADHD need to hear the success stories of those who have used its traits to their advantage (Shankman, 2017).

Similarly, Archer (2014) shares the belief that some entrepreneurs reach their pinnacle of success because of the traits of ADHD, not in spite of them. In fact, he calls ADHD their "superpower." Some of the same traits that can wreak havoc in a classroom setting, such as difficulty sitting still and a limited threshold for tedious tasks, are nonissues to an entrepreneur. In fact, recent research indicates that many ADHDers have the ability to hyperfocus for long periods of time when a project interests them (Flippen, 2020). Archer also contends that individuals with ADHD are often at their best when in a crisis mode or multitasking, a needed skill in running a business. The ADHD brain seeks novelty and new sensations. They are typically not desk-job people. Rather, according to this author, ADHDers are three times more likely to own their own businesses. Some contend that in prehistoric times, those with ADHD were quite possibly the ones out searching for new hunting grounds or scouting new settlements, inspiring the nickname "explorer gene" for the ADHD gene.

In a Harvard Business School study of personality traits, Kerr, Kerr, and Zu (2017) differentiate between traits of entrepreneurs and managers. Entrepreneurs are drawn to environments that are constantly changing, with novel challenges, and are typically more open to new experiences than managers. Rather than just seeing opportunities, they act on them, even in the face of significant risk. While ADHD is never mentioned in the study, the similar traits for success in the entrepreneurial world are interesting to note, such as novelty, risk taking, adventure, and being action-oriented. It adds credence to the high rate of ADHD entrepreneurs.

Successful ADHDers do not always follow the entrepreneurial route. A quick Google search reveals a star-studded cast of individuals with these symptoms who have reached tremendous heights. Gymnast Simone Biles, swimmer Michael Phelps, and singers Adam Levine and Justin Timberlake are just a few. Psychologist John Grohol (2019) contends that many historical figures, including Thomas Edison, Albert Einstein, Wolfgang Mozart, and even Abraham Lincoln seemed to have ADHD symptoms, although of course they were never diagnosed. Some of the strengths these individuals often possess, such as creativity, high intellect, and the ability to hyperfocus on areas of strong interest, can benefit them greatly. Their deficits, such as weak organization and difficulty attending, need support. A tendency toward risk taking could be both a strength and a weakness.

It is vital to realize the potential strengths of these unique individuals as children and adults and to celebrate their stories of success. Conversation in the ADHD community frequently centers on the two sides of ADHD: is it a gift or a curse? The unfortunate reality is that the nature of the disorder often creates substantial obstacles to success. Many do not reach their potential and encounter real struggles in their lives, ranging from academics to mental health issues, addiction, and even incarceration. For the schoolhouse, in particular, putting explorers in desks for seven hours a day can be problematic. But before delving into the challenges, first I discuss what it means to have this disorder.

ADHD: WHAT IT IS, AND WHAT IT ISN'T

First, it's critical to say what ADHD is not. Individuals diagnosed as having the ADHD brain are not lazy or lacking in character, any more than those without it. ADHD is a neurological disorder that is largely genetic. A 2017 study by Sun et al. produced MRI images that demonstrate the differences in ADHD and non-ADHD brains. Visual evidence now shows how ADHD brains are different, even by subtypes—it is not an imagined condition. While estimates vary, the numbers are pretty astounding: Joszt (2017) estimates that 5–8% of children and 4% of adults have it. And according to Fletcher and Wolfe (2009), it's much more common in boys than girls. Although ADHD was once called hyperactivity, not all individuals diagnosed with this neurological condition seem to be hyperactive. Some are quiet individuals who appear lost in their thoughts. We all have moments of inattention, restlessness, and daydreaming—but this is different: it's pervasive, deep, and problematic. And it's real. Telling an ADHD person to just pay attention or try harder is akin to telling someone with two sprained ankles to run faster.

According to the A.D.D. Resource Center (2017), about 6.4 million children have ADHD (the numbers vary). They consider males three times more likely than girls to have ADHD, and those in poverty are also at an increased risk. Boys with ADHD often display symptoms differently than girls. For example, boys might demonstrate more physical symptoms, such as running, hitting, and acting out in general. Girls, on the other hand, might use more verbal aggression, such as teasing, and be the day-dreamers in class. There is also some indication that children of color who present the same symptoms are less likely to be diagnosed than whites. Frye (2017) proposes that this potential underdiagnosis of some groups might have far-reaching effects. A correct diagnosis can result in man-agement of the condition that can change the outcome of academic and career lives. Undiagnosed ADHD, many experts report, can exacerbate other conditions that often occur with ADHD, such as substance abuse, risky behavior, and depression.

Why are boys more likely to have the ADHD brain than girls? Using neuroimaging tools, Rodriquez (2017) studied 128 brain regions in par-ticipants engaged in a task involving concentration. Gender differences emerged. Female brains showed significantly increased activity and blood flow in more areas of the brain, especially in those involving impulse control, focus, mood, and anxiety. Visual and coordination centers were more active in men, with higher levels of blood flow in the cerebellum. These gender-based brain differences are believed to be part of the reason that females have increased rates of Alzheimer's disease and depression. Males have much higher rates of ADHD, behavior-related school incidents, and incarceration.

The ability to sustain attention for long periods of time on tasks of interest or requiring low effort, such as video games or reading, can lead to a false conclusion (Kaufmann, Kalbfleisch, & Castellanos, 2000). After all, how could students who can focus so intensely on some tasks have ADHD? If they can sustain focus on a fascinating science project, for example, why can't they finish a worksheet on adverbs? The real test is to focus on work that is less compelling or interesting. In such situ-ations, the ADHD child has great difficulty regulating and sustaining attention, and often becomes frustrated. ADHD students who are also gifted intellectually often have difficulty staying organized, planning, and predicting consequences of their actions. Kaufmann and colleagues caution that gifted students with ADHD need to learn mechanisms to cope with ADHD traits. In addition, their report, like others, reminds educators and parents of the increased propensity for issues such as substance abuse, depression, and even sleep problems. Some attributes of giftedness may look like ADHD, such as a tendency to eagerly shout out answers and the ability to hyperfocus on tasks of great interest. Daydreaming and divergent/creative thinking might also fall into both categories. Gifted students' aptitude for some tasks can mask ADHD symptoms. Conversely, intellectual gifts may be masked by ADHD behaviors. For example, a student who gazes out the window may be deep in thought or simply distracted. Students who are categorized as both gifted and ADHD may be considered twice exceptional.

The Centers for Disease Control (2019) provides a shortened version of the American Psychiatric Association's *Diagnostic and Statistical Manual of Mental Disorders* that can help diagnose ADHD. Looking at the list of potential symptoms, you might see yourself or someone you know. But symptoms must be present for at least 6 months and at a level that would be deemed inappropriate for the age of the child. There are three types of ADHD. Some individuals are predominantly inattentive, with distractibility, trouble listening to instructions, lack of organization, forgetfulness, and difficulty maintaining attention on tasks. The second type is predominantly hyperactive-impulsive, with difficulty staying seated or being still, excessive talking, difficulty taking turns, and impulsivity. In the third or combined type of ADHD, which is the type most frequently diagnosed, the individual exhibits both sets of characteristics.

When do these traits amount to a disorder? Dr. Russell Barkley (2017) explains that ADHD individuals have extreme amounts of some traits that all humans have. Inattention and difficulty with self-regulation and inhibition are at a point of causing harm or adverse consequences to the individual. Barkley believes that the reasons why some have these traits are largely genetic. In fact, ADHD runs in families almost as much as height. ADHD has a stronger genetic component than IQ, personality traits, or depression. A much smaller percentage develop ADHD through exposure to environment toxins such as lead or mercury, or head trauma. Countless scientific studies have detailed the causes and construction of the ADHD brain. Despite popular notions about sugar consumption, diet, parenting styles, and so on, the science has long been established that ADHD is a diagnosable, legitimate neurological disorder.

Psychiatrist and ADHD expert Dr. Ned Hallowell (n.d.), who diagnosed ADHD in JetBlue's David Neeleman, frequently compares the ADHD brain to the engine of a Ferrari race car, but with bicycle brakes. With the right care, races can be won, but work is needed on strengthening the brakes.

Adults with ADHD may present different symptoms than children. Dr. Hallowell and coauthor Dr. John Ratey (2011) detail criteria for diagnosing ADHD in adults in their best-selling book *Driven to Distraction*. Their first symptom for adult ADHD is a floundering sense of underachievement; the feeling that one cannot get it together or reach one's potential. Other criteria include disorganization, procrastination, difficulty with boredom, a tendency to make inappropriate comments, distractibility or poor focus, a strong need for stimulation, and impatience. Mood swings, chronic low self-esteem, and addiction issues are also on the list. But high levels of creativity and intelligence are often present as well. Most adults will not have every symptom on the list. Again, we all have bouts of impatience, impulsivity, and distractibility, but the ADHD brain has them much more pervasively and chronically.

POTENTIAL IN PERIL: ACADEMICS AND BEYOND

A 2013 study by Kuriyan et al. examined the outlook for children diagnosed with ADHD. Academic and behavioral issues in elementary school, they report, often continue through middle and high school and perhaps even worsen, manifesting as lower grades, course failures, more suspensions and expulsions, increased absenteeism, and a higher dropout rate. These children's relative lack of success as a group continues after high school—they are less likely to enter college, and when they do, they fare worse than non-ADHD peers. They are often underemployed, earn lower wages, and are much more likely to be unemployed. In addition, they are much more likely to be fired and to change jobs frequently.

Students with ADHD are less likely to graduate high school or attend college. Those who make it to the university level, according to a review by Green and Rabiner (2012), earn lower GPAs and are more likely to be on academic probation. The same issues that perhaps plagued them in school, such as managing time and organizing work, are now attempted without family support. They also tend to have lower self-confidence about academics. Emotional issues include difficulty adjusting socially and increased drug and alcohol use. The researchers also cite evidence that, at the college level, prescribed ADHD medications may be misused.

(Other students may even pretend to have ADHD to get the meds!) Perhaps most disheartening, however, is the lack of effective solutions. Green and Rabiner bemoan the lack of available research about the most effective treatments and approaches to supporting ADHD students. The one exception is coaching, which shows promising results.

And while ADHD is often thought of as an educational and behavioral issue, Barbaresi et al. (2013) make the case that it should be looked at much more broadly—as a major health condition. They contend that the majority of individuals with ADHD will deal with at least one mental health problem as adults. Early death from suicide is much higher among ADHD individuals than other groups. Substance abuse and psychiatric disorders are contributing factors. The issues are so prevalent that only a minority of children diagnosed with ADHD will not face adverse outcomes. Their view is that positive outcomes depend on support over a lifetime.

Girls with ADHD specifically were studied over the course of 11 years (Biederman, 2010). These young women exhibited a higher risk of depression, bipolar disorder, bulimia, and antisocial and anxiety disorders. Understanding the higher risks associated with the disorder is important in providing early intervention and ongoing support.

ADHD AND INCARCERATION

Academic issues, mental health concerns, low wages, and increased substance abuse paint a disconcerting picture. Unfortunately, there's more; namely, a significant connection between ADHD and increased engagement in illegal activities. The problem stems from two tracks. First, reduced academic achievement squarely places ADHD students in a high-risk pool of those who are less job ready. Second, some traits, such as impulsivity and risk taking, tend to encourage activities that run counter to the law. One study shared evidence by type of the disorder (Fletcher & Wolfe, 2009). Those with predominantly inattentive ADHD committed more of every crime (except robbery) than those without ADHD. This group is more apt to commit crimes that require some planning, such as drug dealing. Individuals with impulsivity issues , the second type of ADHD, had the greatest number of arrests and convictions. Their crimes were more apt to be impulsive, such as theft. People with ADHD have reduced job opportunities due to their school struggles, which has a general connection to increased criminality. These struggles at school look like a failure to grasp content and include off-task behavior and failing to complete homework. This cycle can result in less positive perceptions by teachers, fewer friends at school, and academic failure. Students with ADHD are more likely to wind up in juvenile facilities, be suspended, and be retained in a grade. They tend to have more traffic violations, particularly speeding. Property theft, carrying concealed weapons, and illegal drug use are all higher in this group. They are also more likely to engage in risky sexual behaviors—and less likely to use contraception.

And while the human cost is the paramount concern, this connection between ADHD and illegal activities comes with a monetary price tag: the same study puts the cost to victims at $50–170 million per year (Fletcher & Wolfe, 2009). The cost to society: somewhere between $2 billion and $4 billion per year. The authors conclude that targeted interventions are needed for this group, who have a greater risk of negative outcomes as adults. However, data on how many of those with ADHD who committed crimes had received treatment for the disorder, either via drugs or behavioral coaching, are lacking. These researchers contend, however, that medication is not enough to manage ADHD.

THE PRISON RESPONSE TO ADHD

The sheer number of prison inmates with ADHD is pretty staggering. Hurley and Eme (2004) estimate that 30–70% of inmates have ADHD. A UK study estimated the rate at 25%, with a worldwide total of ADHD inmates at around 2.8 million (Young et al., 2018). In addition, these authors maintain that ADHD inmates have a higher rate of recidivism, with a two- to threefold higher rate of being arrested again. And more bleak news: incarcerated individuals with ADHD have a higher rate of self-harm, depression, suicide, and substance abuse. While it's hard to find good news in those numbers, here's a sliver of a silver lining: Some prisons have had positive results by treating inmates for ADHD while they are incarcerated. The UK study notes that a multimodal approach to treatment works best, involving both behavioral and pharmacological therapy. Furthermore, they highlight the critical urgency of screening inmates for ADHD. The hopeful part of their data is that effective treatment of ADHD behind bars can substantially reduce future offenses and even conviction rates. These authors strongly advocate for the training of all prison staff, parole officers, and mental health professionals in identifying and treating ADHD for more successful outcomes.

A Delaware prison initiative in which inmates are diagnosed, treated, and coached while incarcerated is revealing (Dopfel, Biden, & Kuprevich, 2013). This project included 140 male inmates, of whom 62.1% screened positive for ADHD. And while just over half (55%) had been diagnosed in the past, none were receiving any pharmacological or behavioral treatment. Demonstrating the incarceration cycle, men in this group had been jailed an average of seven times. That cycle was exacerbated by some of the same difficulties the prisoners, largely men in this study, experienced as boys in school. Their weaker working memories, inattention, and lack of organization can result in a lack of success in following directions by judges, court officials, and police, thus causing more difficulties behind bars—and when they eventually return to their communities. If they are stopped or questioned by police, their inability to follow instructions, accompanied by restlessness and even irritability, sets off red flags. Their genuine forgetfulness can give the appearance that they are fibbing, and their demeanor may come off as noncompliance. Further complicating matters, ADHD inmates are more likely to have co-occurring issues such as mental illness or learning disabilities.

NURTURING ADHD LEARNERS

The propensity for negative outcomes in the ADHD community makes it urgent that we rethink and retool educational practices, because the syndrome's traits run counter to our mode of educational delivery. Imagine a learner who has difficulty sitting still for long, whose brain struggles mightily in completing tedious tasks of little personal interest, who has a natural weakness in following more than a couple of directions at a time, and who is highly distractible. Now, put such students in a large classroom with a plethora of stimuli in which their days are filled with somewhat boring tasks that feel seemingly meaningless—oh, and sit still in a desk for most of seven hours straight while a person at the front of the room talks. Such learners might be able to reconstruct a machine at their kitchen table at night or play master-level chess for hours. They might be the best hockey goalie in town, dodging pucks with amazing accuracy, or perhaps run a small landscaping business out of the garage. The traditional classroom, one could argue, is where they are at their weakest—it makes them square pegs in round holes. A world in which teachers stand and talk and students sit and listen is doable for many kids. They can fill in sheets all day and put them in bins, memorize vocabulary lists, and repeat the information back on Friday. For the ADHD child, school can be a very hard, even humiliating place, one they may not survive.

And obviously, off-task behaviors can frustrate the most diligent and patient of teachers, who are desperately trying to stay on top of curriculum pacing guides and prepare all of their students for high-stakes tests—which often impact teachers' jobs and school rankings. Throughout the day, what ADHD students often hear is: Pay attention, turn around, sit still, pay attention, I already said that, Earth to Josh, pay attention, stop that, turn around, sit still, Space Cadet, stop that, pay attention. . . . Did you take your meds?

ADJUSTING THE SCHOOL EXPERIENCE TO MEET ADHD LEARNERS

Current research indicates that schools must work on multiple fronts—academics, organization, and social-emotional—to stem the negative outcomes. The positive news is that ADHD learners have a lot to offer academically and creatively. Again, these are often our future entrepreneurs, explorers, and adventurers. As one mom recalled, "I had my son take a test to explore careers that would be the best fit for him. I was not happy when one of the top choices was a stuntman. I would prefer that he go into something more along the lines of accounting."

ADHD is somewhat situational—on a soccer field or at a gaming tournament, it might be difficult to discern the child with ADHD traits. These students are wired for movement and novelty, but they require a predictable structure to lessons and protocols. With a teacher who incorporates high-interest tasks, frequent breaks, opportunities for movement, hands-on learning, and choices in work, the learning situation itself can minimize negative occurrences. Conversely, in a more traditional classroom experience where the teacher stands and talks and pupils sit and listen, the innate deficits of the ADHD brain are apt to be accentuated. Therefore, it is imperative that ADHD students be matched with teachers who align with their needs. Sometimes this is not possible, as in smaller schools with one math teacher. In that situation, the teacher needs to alter his or her delivery so that students can access the curriculum. The teachers most beneficial for ADHDers are probably highly effective for all kids.

ADHD typically does not fall under the Individuals with Disabilities Education Act ("IDEA"), which governs the provision of special education services to children who have certain qualifying conditions such as autism, specific learning disabilities, or speech or language impairments, pursuant to individualized education programs ("IEPs"). Rather, students with ADHD are typically offered services under Section 504 of the Rehabilitation Act, under a Section 504 plan. A Section 504 plan is less stringent than an IEP. It provides ways to reduce barriers to learning so that students can access the same curriculum as their classmates alongside them in general education and sometimes gifted classrooms. Therefore, teachers in music, physical education, and art, as well as administrators, need to be in the loop on a student's Section 504 plan. Adjustments listed in 504s for ADHD often include strategies like these:

- Support memory: Strategies might include chunking the lesson into smaller pieces, scaffolding devices, use of visuals and mnemonic devices.
- Facilitate organization: Examples might include planners and apps, agendas, checklists, ensuring that homework is written down, and multimodal instructions. Shortened assignments and additional time may also be included.
- Manage distractions: Items like sitting close to the teacher and away from windows or doors, and partnering with more focused students are examples.
- Provide for movement: These may include stretch breaks or opportunities to work while standing.
- Encourage on-task behavior: These might include age-appropriate rewards for on-task behavior, keeping records of goals and progress by student, and frequent home communication.

Education plans provide a modicum of support for these students and should certainly be carefully implemented and monitored. But many of these items are good practices routinely done by effective teachers. Exemplary teachers don't allow any student to sit for the entire class, yet alone one with a documented medical syndrome. Most educators today, in my observation, already post assignments clearly on the board and on websites, utilize agendas, and chunk material. The point here is that, to maximize the talents of these children, the case can easily be made that the bar needs to be significantly raised beyond the (somewhat generic) guidelines of 504s, which are largely to help a student survive school, rather than thrive. In addition, administrators need to have these kids on their radar—not for behavior, but as students who can be academic achievers and leaders. In light of current research that shows greater academic struggles, more reports of mental health issues, and a higher propensity for incarceration connected to ADHD learners, perhaps approaches beyond things like homework monitoring and frequent breaks are due for consideration (Kuriyan et al., 2013; Green & Rabiner, 2012; Bararesi et al., 2013). Further supports are in order for students who simply cannot absorb content via lectures or passive, tedious work. It will not lift them to their academic potential.

SUPPORTING ADHD LEARNERS

ADHD learners do well in an instructional setting that has enough structure to corral their wandering intellectual gifts but also provides novelty and high interest. Their brains have great difficulty with tedium. Their tendency is to become restless and to wander off-task when doing redundant work that is perceived to have little value or interest. Their best learning experiences have a balance of hands-on activities, movement, and short periods of engaging work. They need to stay productively busy, not idle. Instructions should be explicit and not just spoken, but written as well. Their working memory is often shorter than that of other students, so they can get overloaded with rapid-fire verbal instructions. Chunking tasks is beneficial, so that they can complete a small amount of work and receive positive feedback. For example, they might complete just two math problems rather than an entire sheet. Tomorrow, they may stretch to three or four. This balance of structure and high activity works well for all students—but it is essential for this group.

These are more tweaks than wholesale changes to the lesson planning process. For example, when reading a story to children, give all students a card with a character's name on it. As the story progresses, the children should jot down notes about that character. Next they will go to corners where the character's name is posted. They can share their thoughts about this character. This simple change, rather than expecting them to sit still and listen, can make all the difference for them. They now have an important job to focus on—and something in their hands. When one student is at the board solving a math problem, all students can be engaged by solving the problem at their desks. This minor adjustment keeps the ADHD learner in the game and on-task. During math practice time, allow students the option of working on chart paper on the wall, rather than seated at their desks. In a paired reading setting, the ADHD student can be the scribe who jots down the main idea on a sticky note, gets up, and posts it on the wall. I've observed teachers who have marked areas around all the desks to indicate that students can work anywhere in that area, including standing.

These fascinating learners require compelling, thoughtfully crafted lessons that combine structure yet novelty. Their creative thoughts often need organizational support. Their often-reduced working memory benefits from short bursts of work that they can complete, followed by feedback that they are on the right track. Beyond these small tweaks, the most urgent deficits to be addressed in learning situations are memory, attention deficits, movement, need for novelty and high interest, and lack of organization. Ideas follow for supporting these weaknesses in order to build their academic strengths.

MEMORY STRATEGIES

Memory is a challenge for many students, but particularly for ADHD learners. In the typical day, students experience an onslaught of information. In science, they take notes about the water cycle. Social studies class involves a comparison of different economic systems. By the time math starts, their weary eyes stare at the differences between translations, dilations, and reflections. In language arts, confusion creeps in about who killed a mockingbird. According to Bailey and Pransky (2014), working memory—the part in play during most of class—is quite limited and can get overloaded quickly. One piece that supports learners is connecting the parts, such as leaders, events, or math processes, to the whole, the overarching goal. The authors propose that when students are confused about goals, their working memories pay the price—almost frantically searching for purpose and connectivity.

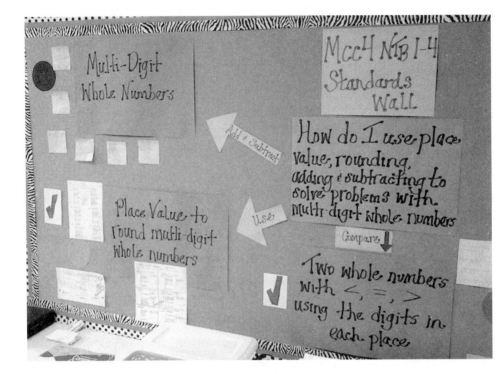

Figure 1.1: STANDARDS WALLS
Source: Susie Maddox, Bleckley County Elementary School

In my books and work, I advocate for something I call standards walls, an anchor graphic organizer that articulates to students how learning targets connect to the central idea, and the path to get there. In the opening minutes of class, the teacher should clarify these clear connections. They are revisited at the close of each learning session—how is your work progressing? Memory is just one benefit of using pictures of goals, rather than isolated essential questions, but retention is a big one. Standards walls support students in organizing a large amount of information, so that they can not only hang on to it but can also clear their brains for more important thinking.

Standards walls consist of a big overarching idea in the center and learning targets to reach that goal. They are planned by unit rather than by daily lessons. The verbs are highlighted—that's the "do" of the target—and the targets are arranged sequentially. Many teachers realize the benefits of checking off targets as the unit progresses to acknowledge progress, as well as posting student work along the way. For the ADHD learner, meeting short-term goals can be motivational—smaller pieces are more doable, and students realize a sense of real accomplishment. These devices bring order to large amounts of information and allow students to see the connections between today, yesterday, and last week. This structure, which can be digital or on paper, puts us all on the same page. For example, Susie Maddox's wall has the central idea about place value and rounding in the center, with targets for meeting success (Figure 1.1). Check marks indicate goals students have met, and their work provides real-time examples.

During the process of mapping out units, it is useful to step back and consider memory items that might pose a barrier to new learning. In math, these might include formulas, place value, steps in a process, multiplication tables, perfect squares, or domain and range. In language arts, the list might include comma rules, figurative language, parts of speech, or prefixes. These lists of prerequisite skills and perhaps vocabulary form the basis of scaffolding.

Scaffolding lifts students up, in the same way that a construction crew creates scaffolding to reach a rooftop. These devices better allow students to concentrate on new content, rather than panicking: "Uh oh, this involves fractions. . . . I'm toast." Instead, we say, "We're going to be working with fractions, but no worries. I've created a bookmark that reminds us how to add two fractions—because, hey, it's been a while, right?" Scaffolding provides a handy reference tool for students. These can actually build self-reliance—students have what they need to be successful right

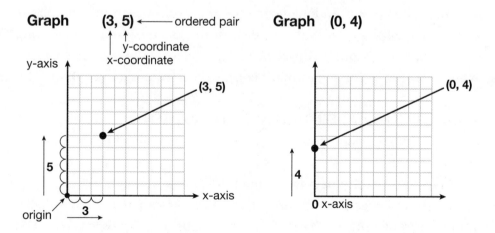

Figure 1.2: SCAFFOLDING
Source: Used with permission of Math in the Fast Lane (https://www.MathinFastLane .com).

in their hands. I heard a masterful teacher recently say this to her class: "For our friends who have not completely memorized multiplication tables, you may use your bookmark with the tables on there. We're still going to work hard on those, but this will speed up your processes today." Scaffolding is tactical and should not be overused. In fact, we want to look for opportunities to fade the scaffolding. But the risk is that students with memory deficits will shut down in frustration without them. The bookmark in Figure 1.2 is for teaching coordinate plane.

Chunking is a strategy that effective teachers employ almost instinctively. Working memories are very limited in terms of what they hold. We would never assign all of the amendments to the Constitution at one time, or a long reading passage to an emerging reader. In science, we might take one or two parts of the circulatory system at a time, present critical information, and allow students time to explore. In all content, providing too many instructions or too much information at once results in off-task behavior or dazed looks because it overloads the memory, which is counterproductive. In our effort to move, move, move, things tend to just spill, spill, spill.

Learning via multiple channels or pathways is more effective for memory retention (Bailey & Pransky, 2014). For that reason, verbal instruction alone brings limits. Incorporating visuals and touch, defending a position, acting out, presenting a case about something—these richer experiences develop a more reliable network of memory. Bailey and Pransky remind us that even long-term memory, from which information is retrieved, may potentially last just days or weeks—the goal is for learning to be permanent. Connecting to prior knowledge is the core of learning. When learners create meaningful connections, retention is enhanced.

STRATEGIES FOR ATTENTION AND ENGAGEMENT

Interest and personal connection are key components of motivation. It's why we put off the dishes, the taxes, and getting the trash to the curb, but have no difficulty paying attention to things we enjoy, like reading, movies, or video games. Building high interest is a particularly important factor in moving an ADHD learner to focus or even hyperfocus. The obvious difficulty is that this is school, not a skateboard park or the Apple store. Our challenge lies in taking an often-dry curriculum and breathing excitement and personal interest into it. The opening minutes of class are just the time for that mission. Again, these strategies make all students stronger, but are essential for the ADHD learner, who has great difficulty maintaining focus and attention.

When I was facilitating a professional development session not long ago, two high school English language arts teachers were busy at our task, which was to create compelling success starters (my name for these) as opposed to bland warm-ups. One was about to teach "The Gift of the Magi," that wonderful short story by O. Henry about the young couple without the funds to obtain gifts for one another. This teacher chose a thought-provoking opener for her students: "What is your most prized possession—and what would it take to part with it?" The other teacher decided to kick off the fiction reading by asking students, "Can people really change?" These brief openers created rich opportunities for students to tap into prior knowledge and personally connect to the text.

For an economics lesson on supply and demand, consider first making a real-world connection. For example, why is it that burrito bars always charge extra for guacamole and not the other ingredients? Students and lovers of this green delight will discover that harvests are down (supply) while demand has skyrocketed. Some restaurants have even resorted to making fake guacamole, using a similar-tasting squash as a substitute. Business owners are faced with either increasing prices, finding substitutes, or removing guacamole from their menus. What would you do as a restaurant owner in light of this crisis? This real-world example adds personal relevance to the upcoming task and even taps into being a business owner. In math, if students are studying rounding or estimating, business examples can enhance relevance. For example, you could say, "You are a business owner with a busy schedule today, but you want to get a quick look at how your month is going. You tap on your phone banking app. Estimate your income and expenses for the month with these numbers. . . ." Real-world relevance is all around students. For example, "I just got a notice from my cell phone provider that I only have 10% remaining on my data plan until my bill date next Tuesday. Help me figure out how to allocate my data without having to pay an overage fee." Real-world relevance, relatability, and tapping into prior knowledge bring focus and interest, a critical need for ADHD learners.

A beautifully engaging technique that is safe for everyone, but especially perfect for ADHD learners, is called sorting. For example, if students are preparing to read Daniel Pink's book *When*, which is about how the time of day affects us, students might first predict (a critical reading skill) which of these are facts and which are fibs. Crafting them on strips of paper makes this a tactile exercise, which enhances memory and engagement. As pair or groups discuss what they know about time and personal performance, intellectual curiosity builds about the subject. Now, as the text unfolds, students revisit their earlier decisions. Sorts are for every subject. In math, students can sort irrational and rational numbers; in social studies, they could sort characteristics of colonies.

Create Three Columns: Fact, Fib, No Clue

- More surgery-related mishaps occur in the afternoons than mornings.
- You're more likely to get prison time with an afternoon hearing.
- Most traffic accidents occur between 2:00 and 4:00 PM.
- The most unproductive time of day is 3:30 PM.
- Morning math classes typically have higher test scores and grades.
- High school students do better with a later start time.

Real-world relevance enhances learning throughout the lesson, but the opening minutes have the power to draw ADHD students into learning with compelling connections to improve attention and motivation. Class starts off on a positive, successful note. Compare this approach to going over homework. For ADHD students, completing homework and finding it in their overflowing backpacks can be a real challenge. Even at school, with all the supports provided, completing work is a real challenge. Now, the expectation is for ADHD learners to head home to accomplish this on their own. Yes, they should do their homework. But do we want to start off their classroom experience today on that unsuccessful note? By comparison, success starters provide opportunities right out of the gate to be successful, to join in, to share experiences. That early success provides opportunities for commendation. "I love that answer you just gave about symmetry in construction." Deeper into the lesson, when students are working in groups or independently, may be a better time to survey (or help locate) their homework.

The teacher-talk portion of the lesson should be short, with urgently needed information. In addition, visuals should support the talking. The question becomes: What do we need to teach explicitly and what can students explore on their own? The teacher talking is typically the most passive element of the lesson for all students, because educators are delivering the work. Even with a short lesson, chunking is needed. For example, explain nonrenewable energy first. Next, on their individual whiteboards, students write two characteristics of nonrenewable energy. Students can then hold up their responses or share with a partner. Thus renewable energy is explained. After this part, students can be provided sticky notes for creating Venn diagrams comparing renewable and nonrenewable and post those on the wall. To support focus, provide a job for ADHD students to do during the mini lesson. "Russell, I have three things I'm going to share about the sun today. Would you please check them off as I complete them?" Or let him be the tech support person during the teacher lesson.

Using short, often distributed, mini lessons enables the work to move quickly to students' shoulders. Teaching continues, but this student-centered model allows conversations at tables and with partners, closer to students where teachers can have some eye contact and personal engagement. Often, the ADHD student will need to have spoken instructions repeated; therefore, it's essential that instructions be visual as well.

STATION TEACHING AND ADHD LEARNERS

Station teaching with ADHD students might sound a bit daunting, but this approach can bridge their deficits quite well. The key is structure, modeling, and preparing them for transitions. Stations incorporate novelty, movement, different learning channels, and short tasks. Reading can be broken up via stations. Rather than simply shortening reading (or math) lessons, it is helpful to prioritize the most important things students need to accomplish. For example, consider starring or highlighting the most important paragraphs. Then announce to all students, "There's a good chance you might not have time to finish all of the reading. Don't stress about it—just read the starred paragraphs." Using stations, a student might sort in one, practice a few problems in another, and respond in writing at the next. Having said that, it is imperative that the learning target is the focus of every station, rather than being activity-based.

An additional critical element of station teaching is this: What does every student know? In stations, students can rely heavily on other students—everyone looks busy, but what are they learning? Here are two ways to incorporate individual accountability. First, include an anchor activity that students carry with them. This is work that they engage in during available minutes, such as math problems. In other subjects, it might be an error analysis or an essay with missing pieces. Second, include a simple graphic organizer, with a section for each station. In addition to the group task, students have something to do in each box, such as doing one math problem on their own, or giving a written summary or their opinion about something they have read. One last tip: it's helpful to include answer keys at stations, so that students get quick feedback, because having students wait for teacher feedback can bring restlessness.

Here is an example of a review station I use for the branches of government that is effective for all students, but works particularly well for students with attention issues. This lesson is available for everyone at www .MyEdExpert.com. (After going to the site, type in Suzy Pepper Rollins in the search bar.) Station 1: A foundational sort with the headings legislative, executive, and judicial. Station 2: A blog with errors students locate. Station 3: A card game with clues on PowerPoint. Students get three cards to play: executive, legislative, and executive. Station 4: A fact/fib exercise. The anchor activity is an essay with missing pieces they complete as they have extra minutes.

STUDENT CHOICES WITHIN LESSONS

Choice can be a strong motivator. (Who would frequent a restaurant with no options?) Incorporating choices can spur ADHD students to action, because some might play perfectly to their strengths. For example, they could create a business plan, draw a cartoon, or record a video on their phones. They could select from three writing prompts or two reading selections. In math, if 10 problems are presented, let them choose six. They could read with a partner, in the teacher circle, or on their own. While reading, they could make sticky notes, use a highlighter, or place colorful dots on important parts. In language arts, they could select one of four novels, rather than being required to read a specific book. Menus, sometimes called choice boards, provide structure to choices. These can be arranged like a menu, with appetizers, entrees, and dessert, by points, or by category. Learners select their options and earn points. The menu

Figure 1.3: MENU OF STUDENT CHOICES

TOPIC	CHOICE A	CHOICE B	CHOICE C
Who represents you?	Create a short video explaining to citizens of your state who represents them.	Create a chart for new voters depicting who represents them. Include websites and voting maps.	Draw a graphic for a newspaper's website showing who represents them.
Separation of powers	Create a foldable or flip chart that demonstrates the responsibilities of each branch of government.	Create a graphic organizer that details the responsibilities of each branch of government.	Create a children's book that explains the branches of government.
Checks and balances	Create an original diagram that demonstrates checks and balances.	Create a slide show that demonstrates checks and balances.	Write one page of a textbook that explains checks and balances.

in Figure 1.3 on the branches of government would nicely accompany the stations above. Learners can demonstrate their understandings in varying ways.

Supporting the attention and engagement of ADHD learners is about providing opportunities for them to accentuate their strengths, while tweaking lessons and assignments to accommodate their deficits. An approach that incorporates lessons of high interest and connectivity, shorter work segments, and often hands-on tasks work well with these learners. When educators worry about potential off-task behaviors, there can be a tendency to keep them in desks busy with seat work as a prophylactic measure. But remaining seated for long periods of time trying in vain to focus on a tedious task can be counterproductive and can even backfire. In the same vein, recess may be the best part of the ADHD student's day, so there's a temptation to punish off-task behavior with a reduction of physical activity, hoping the unpleasantness will reduce the behaviors. But frustration can swell and spill over for ADHD students.

These students need recess more than anyone else. The astute educator will watch for cues from students and take action. "Let's get out of those desks and take a stretch break!" One teacher I observed recently said to an elementary student, "Would it be helpful for you to walk around a bit?" The girl nodded. "Perfect. I've got a note I need delivered to Ms. Baker— would you take it?" I have no idea what was on that note, but I suspect it was something like, "Hey, there. We just need a break."

STRUCTURES

Structure is critical to ADHD students and adults, although this may seem inconsistent with their need for novelty, high interest, and movement. Their success depends on the balance between these factors. Adults in the ADHD community talk about their structures for success, like keeping their closets arranged, calendars, planners, computer apps, and multiple timers. In other words, the structures we teach our ADHD kids now will hopefully lay the groundwork for crafting their own structures as they get older. The word *structure* can sound like something boring, or even controlling. This is different. These devices are meant to support learning at a higher level. These structures help students better cope with an environment that is full of distractions. Again, your classroom will include 20-something other students who also need and deserve attention. These structures help to lasso students' thoughts to prioritize the jobs they need to do.

While everyone benefits from external structures—routines, schedules, predictability—our ADHD students need them more than others. Hallowell and Ratey explain it perfectly: "They need external structure so much because they so lack internal structure. They carry with them a frightening sense that the world might cave in at any moment . . . on the brink of disaster, as if they were juggling a few more balls than they're able to" (2011, p. 112). These structures help keep students organized, on schedule, in the right place at the right time, and help with prioritizing the order of things to tackle. Structures can bring a "sigh of relief" (p. 112) to ADHD learners—their world seems more in control. At an age-appropriate level, it is helpful to let the students help create them.

A common structure in the classroom is the agenda. This list is checked off as we go and helps support focus and behavior. For example, Figure 1.4 is a simple one from a math lesson. The last item is homework, to be

Figure 1.4: DAILY AGENDAS PROVIDE A PREDICTABLE STRUCTURE
FOR STUDENTS

★	Success Starter: The deer are eating my garden. I need a fence!
★	Mini lesson with notes
★	Practice: Perimeter problems in pairs
★	3 problems on your own
★	Close: 1 problem
★	Take pics or sketch 3 examples of perimeters in your neighborhood

checked the next day. Just the action of checking off a box when something is complete can bring a sense of accomplishment. ADHD learners are the perfect students to be the box checkers!

Some students benefit from having class notes either made or partially outlined. A long essay, for example, may require a graphic organizer with frames for introduction, body, and conclusion. If the lesson includes a foldable or flip chart, it's helpful to have a couple already made, just in case. Organizational structures are essential, such as color-coded folders for subjects. For example, yellow like the sun could be for science; the math folder, magenta. Planners and calendars are beneficial, as well as a mechanism for ongoing contact with home. Longer projects require structures with time lines that include frequent checks by adults. To ask an ADHD student to turn something in a month from now without support along the way will yield a predictable outcome. Longer assignments certainly need parental communication, so that this is on the family's radar.

There are also many computer apps for students and adults with ADHD, including to-do lists, prizes when chores are completed, mind mapping, and an app that will pester the user until a task is complete. With one app, students take pictures of their notes, and the application stores them so they won't lose them. With one called 30/30, the student creates a task and assigns a time for completion, and then the timer begins. The novelty of these apps might be a perfect fit for some ADHD learners. Doyle (2019) has reviewed some of the more interesting apps.

These structures help students with organization, prioritization, and on-task behavior. But structures are not controls—students with ADHD will learn to resist controls. In addition, many teachers utilize positive behavioral structures that reward students for staying on task, completing their own work, working well within groups, and waiting their turn—challenging arenas for these children. A common thread in reading about adults with ADHD is a nagging perception, sometimes even anger, that teachers did not view them favorably. With the need for frequent redirections and teachers often hovering around their desks, this should not come as a surprise.

Behavioral structures should be as positive as possible. Set goals with students and commend them when they reach them. Ten minutes of solid work today may develop into a goal of 12 tomorrow. Completed work may allow them extra recess time or whatever rewards your school supports. Allow a student to be the line leader or the row captain or the math app queen. It's a good idea in general to give these kids jobs to do on a regular basis—jobs that require them to move, even as simple as passing out papers. It's advisable to ignore minor off-task behaviors as much as possible. When possible, visit with them at lunch or at after-school events, activities other than academics. Seeing them in an arena in which they shine might provide a broader perspective on their gifts. As much as possible, their toughest coursework should be in the beginning of the day.

HOME CONNECTIONS

Working closely with parents of ADHD students can help students stay on track. Teachers do not diagnose ADHD in children—that is largely the domain of pediatricians. In fact, teachers have probably been trained not to mention that a child may possess this syndrome. Teachers, however, are often the ones who relay to parents that their children are experiencing difficulties in class. In the classroom setting, a set of skills is an asset to learners, such as sustained attention, ability to follow a series of instructions, finishing tasks, listening, and remembering things. Therefore, a student who may be one of the brightest in class may be underachieving due to deficits in these areas. The near-constant redirection by the teacher to a child to stay on task, turn around, or stop a behavior can wear on a child's self-esteem and perceptions of school. The addition of poor grades on top of a sense that "the teacher doesn't like me" can fuel school frustration. A teacher's concern often marks the beginning of the process of discerning why the child is having difficulty in school. These concerns may seem to contradict the child's behavior at home. The child may, for example, work well at the kitchen table one-on-one with few distractions. The child may exhibit times of hyperfocus, such as when gaming, or immersed in a movie, or at a martial arts class.

For parents, the first two important steps when concerns arise are to secure an accurate diagnosis and to educate oneself. The problem might be ADHD or something else. A game plan can be developed for the child, but a correct diagnosis comes first. When a student is diagnosed with ADHD, support organizations can be helpful to families. Children and Adults with Attention-Deficit/Hyperactivity Disorder (CHADD, https://chadd.org/) is a nonprofit organization that offers support for families, ranging from courses to an online community and resource directories. Many areas have support groups connected to CHADD. Another online support resource is ADDitude, whose website includes support articles, podcasts, and resources (https://www.additudemag.com/). In addition, there are a multitude of books and online resources about ADHD. Immersion in understanding ADHD will help parents become active team members with school leaders, teachers, counselors, and coaches.

Encourage parents to build a team of support around their child, which can include administrators, athletic and instructional coaches, and especially the school counselor. Counselors often possess training in behavior therapy, an important aspect in the successful treatment of ADHD, and can provide resources to classroom teachers and administrators for positive strategies for a child's success. Counselors may serve as the child's unofficial ADHD coach, as well as providing professional development for the school staff. School counselors can act as a bridge between home and school and can provide connections to other supports in your community. In addition, counselors can explore careers for ADHD students and talk about how traits that sometimes make school a tough place can actually be an advantage in the real world.

ADHD can impact the entire family. *Driven to Distraction* (Hallowell & Ratey, 2011) is a compelling, best-selling book to share with parents. The authors—both medical doctors—use composite stories of children and adults they have treated to detail a cycle that often emerges at home. For example, if a child does not complete chores or homework, parents may respond with tighter restrictions on behavior. These additional control measures can result in defiance, sometimes exacerbating the situation. Siblings who might be doing all that's being asked of them notice the amount of attention funneled to the ADHD child, who could be labeled the "bad kid," further fueling issues. ADHD families often need support, such as counseling.

UNCOVER THEIR STRENGTHS

Many ADHD experts recommend physical exercise as therapeutic for ADHD kids; in fact, it can even reduce symptoms by regulating dopamine and norepinephrine in the brain. Physical exercise can help them be more successful in class—using recess or gym class as leverage for better behavior is ill advised. Which sports and activities are viewed as the best fit for ADHD kids? According to the editors of the support website ADDitude (2015), swimming is one good choice. Swimming provides opportunities for personal growth as students work to improve their speed. Olympic champion and ADHD advocate Michael Phelps widely credits swimming for improving his focus and discipline. Martial arts are often a good fit as well, as children master levels by a combination of following instructions with physical exercise and routines. Wrestling, tennis, gymnastics, and track are others. Soccer and baseball can fit as well, but experts caution about sports in which the child will have to sit on the bench for long periods of time. Athletic coaches benefit from information about working with ADHD athletes, such as giving them a job to do during down time. Sports and hobbies should be anxiety releasers, not spur additional stress. Be it sculpting or woodworking or playing the drums, it's critically important for teachers, coaches, leaders, and parents to find something that builds them (Editors of ADDitude, 2015).

Another hobby that could be a perfect fit might be a surprise: chess.

In 2014, ElDaou and El-Shamieh reported that implementing a chess program with ADHD students resulted in increased focus, more control, and slightly improved listening skills. They observed students taking longer to think about their moves and increased concentration. While more research is needed here, their observations mirror what I have observed personally after beginning morning chess sessions in my homeroom. It began with a couple of chessboards for students who arrived early. News spread quickly and the group expanded, which led to a need for organization, which led to competitive tournaments. High school coaches heard about the competition and joined in. Students got better and better and arrived earlier and earlier. Some of our students beat the seasoned chess players and grown coaches—this thing got serious. Rule books were secured, and one nonsanctioned wrestling match ensued on my classroom floor. (Thankfully, our wrestling coach was on hand playing that morning.) And while chess can be played online against opponents all over the world, the board game became a social outlet for students and a chance to shine at something other than sports. I believe that it mattered greatly to them that the coaches came—they got to show off a bit in a different venue. An especially poignant side effect was the patience these students demonstrated in teaching other students how to play chess—they genuinely wanted to share their love of the game.

RESEARCH TO PRACTICE

ADHD learners are a particularly vulnerable group. From academic failure to disciplinary actions to mental health issues, this group needs wrap-around support from teachers, leaders, counselors, and parents. The prison research cited earlier (Hurley & Erme, 2004, Young et al., 2018) gave various numbers of exactly how many inmates have ADHD. But if estimated percentages are reliable, just in the United States that equates to somewhere between 600,000 and 1,400,000 inmates. ADHD is the most diagnosed disorder in children—this is a large group of students who need strategic support. To address the potential negative outcomes that may befall these students requires work on multiple fronts: academic, organizational, social-emotional, and home. In addition, schools should make every effort to be welcoming to these children, to include them and find areas of involvement, so that they can feel more positive about

Figure 1.5: PRACTICES THAT INCREASE OR DECREASE SUPPORT
TO ADHD LEARNERS

PRACTICES THAT INCREASE SUPPORT	PRACTICES THAT DECREASE SUPPORT
Chunking tasks	Long assignments without breaks
Movement (standing to work, stations, hands-on learning, recess)	Sitting for long teacher talks; using gym or recess as leverage for classroom behaviors
Scaffolding (memory, structure, organization)	One-size-fits-all instruction
High-interest, personally relevant tasks	No choices, low-value tasks
Involvement in extracurricular activities	Entire focus on academics, their weak spot
Structures for organization	No support for organization
Consistent parental communication	Inconsistent expectations between home and school
Leaders, coaches, and counselors on support team	All on teachers' shoulders
Uncovering strengths	Deficit driven

their learning environment. These learners can quite honestly exhaust teachers and parents. But the urgency requires new solutions, increased resolve, and thoughtful ideas.

Myths and stigmas about ADHD linger—that it means a lack of discipline at home, poor diet, defiance, or laziness. Understanding current research is important in shifting our mind-sets about this medical condition in order to better support students. Today's reality of pacing guides, benchmarks, and high-stakes tests can create almost a panicked push by teachers throughout the day. All students deal with a bombardment of information and concepts coming at them, but our ADHD kids are more likely to falter with this approach. A close home–school partnership is essential for ADHD students to realize success.

The founder of JetBlue contends that many students with this disorder are essentially thrown out of the school boat (Shankman, 2017). School can indeed be turbulent waters for these kids. While they may be born entrepreneurs or adventurers, their academic and emotional paths are often fraught with struggles. As educators, we must create a welcoming spot for these unique individuals. One of the most important and cherished aspects of school is diversity—and that extends to our ADHD students. First, we must see their strengths. Second, we must create supports that can help them over the course of their lives.

Figure 1.5 is a quick reference of ideas on practices to increase and decrease for ADHD learners.

QUESTIONS TO PONDER

- Is the balance between meeting educational targets and the emotional needs of the child appropriate?
- Does each ADHD learner have a support team?
- Are administrators building positive relationships with ADHD learners?
- Are instructional strategies appropriately adjusted to meet their needs?
- Are students being punished by withholding physical exercise?
- Are ADHD learners provided opportunities to display their strengths?
- Are homework length and/or time lines being adjusted?
- Do long-term projects include structures, checks, and time lines?
- Are students encouraged to participate in extracurricular activities?
- Are behavior plans positive in nature?
- Are parent–teacher partnerships strong for ADHD learners?

MOVING FORWARD

➤ What efforts can be made in your building to support ADHD learners academically and socially? _____
_____
_____
_____
_____

CHAPTER 2

Tough in Any Language

"Today, class, we are going to explore mathematical models and generate diagrams to compare and contrast electric and gravitational forces between two charged objects." Yikes. That's daunting in English. Now imagine hearing this science lesson in words other than your home language. Just to understand the learning target, students need to possess this vocabulary: models, generate, diagrams, compare, contrast, electric, gravitational, forces, and charged. For a student trying to learn English as well as physics, this is a steep academic climb. During the next period, a Charles Dickens novel is introduced. After lunch: a deep dive into colonialism.

And then there are instructions they must process, with the sometimes-tricky English language. For example, "Let's table that conversation for another time. Now, on your tables are supplies for our unit on the periodic table. You will be constructing a table, so you'll need your tablets." It's no wonder that a teacher once shared with me that it was midyear before she realized that her English language learners (ELLs) had a big misconception about whole numbers. They thought that whole numbers were the ones with holes in them, like 6, 8, and 9.

Language barriers are but one issue, albeit a big one. Sitting in a classroom one day, a student asked the teacher, "When are we going to study something about where *I'm* from?" A simple, yet profound question. Every educator knows about the importance of connecting students' prior knowledge and to new information. This girl was waiting patiently for those moments. The problem for the teacher was that the class was a required state history course. The standards were clearly about this student's new home, not her place of origin. Yet even within that context connections could readily be made. Many things, such as geographical features, types of government, civil rights issues, and agriculture are universal in nature.

Learning a new language. Adjusting to a new culture. Passing coursework. Taking high-stakes tests in a second language. Graduating high school. Being adequately prepared for college. The challenges ELLs shoulder at school are weighty indeed. How frustrating it must be to not be able to shine at content knowledge simply because the words are not there to demonstrate understanding of information—or even just to share ideas with a teacher or classmate.

SCOPE

English language learners are the fastest-growing group of students in the United States. As of fall 2016, 4.9 million or 9.6% of students were considered ELLs in the United States (National Center for Education Statistics, 2019). By comparison, there were 3.8 (8.1%) in the fall of 2000. Therefore, in 16 years, roughly a million additional children now require support for English proficiency and content mastery. In California, over 20% of students are ELL, and Texas is not far behind with 17.2%. Other states, such as Montana and Vermont, have much smaller student enrollments—both around 2% (National Center for Education Statistics, 2019). By far, the dominant language spoken at home—over 76%—is Spanish, but there are many other languages as well, including a significant number of Chinese and Arabic speakers. According to the Kids Count Data Center (2018), 22% of children today speak a language other than English at home. New Jersey, for example, realized an increase in the past decade from 5% to 30% of all children; California's rate of 44% is the highest. Per the U.S. Department of Education (n.d.) over 400 languages are spoken in U.S. homes. And while only a handful of languages is represented in some states, such as Mississippi, Pennsylvania has 225.

HOW ARE SCHOOLS ADJUSTING TO CHANGES
IN STUDENT POPULATIONS?

How are schools responding to the increase in students with different language needs? Some regions of the country are playing catch-up. Indiana experienced a 409% growth rate in ELL populations over a 10-year period (Brooks, Adams, & Morita-Mullaney, 2010). However, they only had 325 certified English as a second language (ESL) teachers in the entire state, resulting in a ratio of 143:1. The growth reflects not only an increase in immigrants but changes in where they settle. More are settling in rural and suburban areas, with more than half outside of urban areas (Jensen, 2006). These areas may be less apt to have appropriate supports than cities like New York that have a long history of immigration. Sanchez (2017) reports that in 2016, 32 states reported not having enough teachers for ELLs, the federal government identified over 100 school districts in which somehow not a single student was receiving additional support for ELL, and over a half million students were not receiving any additional help at school to learn English. This report echoes new migration patterns as well, noting that states like Arkansas, Kentucky, and both Carolinas have experienced the greatest growth.

Quintero and Hansen (2017) contend that teacher programs have lagged behind in preparing educators for these changes. They report that 30 states do not require any training for general education teachers in effective practices for ELLs. And while the focus is often on students new to the English language, they emphasize that the majority of ELLs are second-generation immigrants—they were born in the U.S. but do not use English predominantly at home. Consider this statistic in light of a National Center for Education Statistics (NCES) survey given to more than 3 million teachers that revealed that over half had at least one ELL in their classroom—and that survey was in 2012.

Training for teachers on how to effectively support ELLs in reaching academic and language goals has often been sparse, or nonexistent. A large number of students are receiving no additional support. How are English learners faring as a group? With these current dynamics in play, one could argue that the results will be predictably disappointing.

POTENTIAL IN JEOPARDY

By many measures, our English learners are not reaching their academic potential. One out of every 10 students in the U.S. today is learning English, a total of almost 5 million children. The high school graduation rate for this group is a disappointing 63% nationwide. One state, however, with a large ELL population, has a graduation rate of just 37%. Far fewer ELLs take college entrance exams than other students. And while 7.3% of students in general are identified for gifted programs, just 2% of ELLs are enrolled (Sanchez, 2017). Furthermore, Kanno and Cromley (2015) report that only 19% of ELLs will advance to four-year colleges, compared to 43% of monolingual students. In addition, of those who enter postsecondary education, just 12% completed a four-year program within eight years. Why? In their view, English learners are often not being enrolled in college preparatory courses. In the same vein, Callahan, Wilkinson, and Muller (2010) believe that the emphasis on raising high school graduation rates might be resulting in a tendency to place ELL students in basic courses at the expense of more advanced college-preparatory courses. Educators and counselors should be aware that ELLs who are interested in attending a four-year school are less likely even to complete the application process than other students.

The dismal news is that there is a 40% gap in fourth grade reading scores and eighth grade math scores between ELL and non-ELL students (Murphey, 2014). In fact, just one-third of ELL students scored Basic or above on the National Assessment of Educational Progress (NAEP) math test, compared with 75% of non-ELL students. In only three states did a majority of ELL students meet this basic measure in math. In five states, less than 20% of these students met even the Basic level in math. (NAEP scores are categorized by Basic, Proficient, and Advanced.)

I observed the reality behind this research in a fifth-grade math class. A passionate teacher halfway through teaching standards in a rural district had received two new students within a month's time. Neither student spoke any English—one spoke Russian; the other, Spanish. With no ESL coteacher and no specialized training, she was also under pressure to produce high test scores. Left to her own devices, she valiantly used phone apps and videos to supply what she could for the math standard in their native languages. She whispered to me, "What am I supposed to do?" Later, in a town three hours from hers, I was doing learning walks in a building with a leader. A fifth grade science teacher rushed into the hallway to talk to us. His urgent words: "I have a new student from Guatemala who speaks no English. . . . I teach *science*." In other words, he needed help. And I recall observing a young man in an urban middle school class at midyear. He could speak some English but could not read or write in any language—his formal education could be counted in months, not years. Shortly after his arrival, the state writing test was given. He quietly doodled on the paper. A week later, he disappeared from the school.

Five million students. Low graduation and college entry rates. Large gaps in academic progress. And while the federal government does gather information about how ELL students are faring, the bulk of education funding comes from state and local levels, with only about 11% provided by the federal government (Sanchez, 2017). Looking at the dismal academic progress of this group of children as a whole, whatever we are collectively doing as a nation is not working very well.

YOU TEACH THEM ENGLISH; I'LL HANDLE CHEMISTRY

Consider the difficulty of understanding a lecture on feudalism or reading a textbook about chemical reactions or a play by Shakespeare when the words spoken or written are in a foreign language. The solution may seem logical: if someone else could just teach the English part first, the content would come easier. But according to an overview on language acquisition stages, it takes between 5 and 7 years to reach advanced fluency in a new language if students have strong first-language literacy skills (Robertson & Ford, n.d.). For students who lack first-language skills, it takes 7 to 10 years to reach that level. While ESL teachers often provide some pull-out language support, it takes time to learn a new language, and when students are pulled from the content class to learn English, other students are moving forward on critical content.

It's helpful for general education teachers and leaders to have a basic understanding of the stages of language acquisition. This knowledge enhances understanding of why students might respond (or not) to questions in the hallway or might be achieving below our expectations. The following summary of stages (Robertson & Ford, n.d.) demonstrates how language abilities develop in social settings first, rather than academic ones. This explains why teachers hear students conversing in English in the lunchroom or hallway, but not in social studies or science class, and why students might appear reticent when asked an academic question in class or might need additional time to gather a response. At lunch, the conversation is social and does not require academic vocabulary. Students can select words they know. They are likely not discussing how rocks are classified at the lunch table.

In simple terms, here are the stages of language acquisition:

1. For around the first six weeks, students are in a preproduction period, in which they just take words in and make few attempts at speaking the new language.
2. Largely still just listening, students may attempt a few words or phrases, but often with errors in this early production period.
3. Students speak more frequently, and longer sentences emerge. Vocabulary improves; however, the speaker shows more comfort with familiar topics in this speech-emergent stage.
4. Social speech improves in this beginning fluency stage, but academic conversations prove challenging due to vocabulary.
5. Students can now communicate with fluency and engage in higher-order thinking conversations in the new language. They speak well in social settings but still have gaps in vocabulary and understanding expressions in this intermediate fluency stage.
6. Comfortable in their second language, students can manage new content and context at this advanced fluency stage.

Different English learners will be in different places in their new language mastery continuum. A general impression of students' language acquisition supports an array of instructional decisions in the classroom, particularly in flexible grouping. For example, if students are being asked to defend a position on economic models, consider pairing a student at the listening stage with an English learner who demonstrates more fluency. If the task involves playing a vocabulary card game, it might be appropriate to pair two students who are in the beginning stages of language development with one set of beginning cards, and engage a different pair with more challenging words. Erben, Ban, and Casteneda (2009) emphasize that, while English learners might be adept at conversational language, academic literacy is much more difficult.

What language should students speak, read, or write in while processing and demonstrating what they know about classroom content? It can be a bit unnerving for teachers to hear conversations in class in different languages. Are they talking about the content? Laughter might erupt in a group, and instincts tell us to clamp it down as off-task behavior. It is entirely appropriate and beneficial for students to utilize their home languages in making sense out of new content. In fact, Fenner and Snyder (2017) contend that incorporating home languages—even if that language is not spoken by the teacher—can benefit English literacy while supporting a welcoming cultural environment. Ferlazzo and Sypnieski (2018) add that students' use of their home languages helps them learn English and supports reading comprehension. Furthermore, they caution teachers against banning home languages, which can diminish the classroom environment. Learning new content in their home language can increase students' understanding in both languages (Erben et al., 2009). And while the general education teacher likely does not speak the learner's home language, there are strategies, including use of technology, that can support the use of home languages. This might involve something as simple as short, timed breaks with elbow partners to summarize or construct opinions about what was just taught, in any language. Or students might write a few sentences in English and a few in their first language. The fifth grade math teacher with just two ELLs in her room who spoke two different languages incorporated math videos in the students' home languages to support the instruction provided in English. Google Translate is another standby option to bring in first languages to help support acquisition of new content.

Educators should not assume that students can read and write well in their first language. Students may have limited or interrupted formal education (Ferlazzo & Sypnieski, 2018). If students have received sporadic formal education (such as the young man in my class mentioned earlier) and possess low literacy in their heritage language, it will likely impact how quickly they can become proficient in their second language.

Understanding students' literacy levels in their home language impacts instructional decisions about how to scaffold content. One student, for example, may be adept with a glossary in the home language to fill in missing pieces, or a translated piece of text. A student who has reading difficulties in the first language will not be as successful with that approach. Therefore, it is essential to learn as much as possible about students who are learning English to better guide instructional decisions and to build teacher-student connections.

MODELS OF INSTRUCTION FOR ENGLISH LANGUAGE LEARNERS

A continuum of instructional models exists to help students learn rigorous academic content while becoming proficient in English. Factors that impact district designs of programs include the nature and characteristics of learners and resources available, such as the availability of ESL teachers (Erben et al., 2009). In a pull-out program, students leave their classrooms to focus specifically on English skills. While they are out of the room, of course, they are missing the academic content other students are receiving. More schools today encourage a more inclusive model of learning, in which students stay put with their classmates, and the ESL teacher provides supports within the content classroom (Fenner & Snyder, 2017). However, increased accountability for content knowledge combined with more English learners and limited numbers of ESL teachers have often resulted in placing ELL students in instructional situations with few modifications for their special learning needs. This submersion approach may not take into account students' level of proficiency or period of time since arrival (Erben et al., 2009). In other words, content teachers are increasingly likely to have ELLs in their classrooms who need language support, without the help of an ESL teacher.

ELL models range from pull-outs and push-ins, to teaching young students in their home language first and then transitioning to English coteaching, to dual language immersion. There are hybrids as well; for example, I taught science in a district in which a Spanish-speaking paraprofessional supported students in my class by translating science content, largely vocabulary. Dual language immersion is yielding positive results in some districts. A study of 1,625 students in Portland public schools tracked the progress of students in dual language immersion classes from

2004 through 2013 (Steele et al., 2017). The researchers note that students in the program outscored other students in reading in grade five by 13% and in grade eight by 22%. The growth rate equals about seven months in grade five and nine months in grade eight. No difference was seen in math or science. In dual language classes, native English speakers are mixed with ELLs and the content is taught in approximately a 50-50 mix. Classes might be taught by coteachers or an individual bilingual teacher. Students in this model learn from one another, with the goal of all students in the classroom becoming bilingual. To see how one district is implementing this approach in kindergarten and first grades, take a look at this website for Dallas Independent School District's Dual Language Program (https://www.dallasisd.org/duallanguage).

STRATEGIES FOR TEACHING CONTENT TO ENGLISH LEARNERS

For the general education content teacher with rigorous standards and rapid-fire pacing, creating content learning experiences that also build language acquisition can feel like a lot. The good news from the research is that instructional practices that build success in English learners, such as increased modeling and incorporating visuals, can enhance learning for all students. In addition, many content literacy strategies that support English learners might already be embedded in instructional practices.

The following sound general principles are readily implemented in the general education classroom. The first four come from a handbook (downloadable) on models and teaching strategies for ELLs (Moughamian, Rivera, & Francis, 2009). The remaining three are mine.

- Incorporate visual elements throughout your lessons. Photos of mountain ranges or amphibians are more powerful than simply talking about them. Include manipulatives when appropriate, such as in math, science, and art.
- Slow your speaking pace down and enunciate clearly. Incorporate simple written instructions, such as a lesson agenda, so that students are not relying only on speech. Clarity is enhanced when students can see gestures and facial expressions, so minimize the time you spend with your back turned.

- Incorporate students' background knowledge and experiences into your lessons.
- Integrate effective academic vocabulary instruction and literacy strategies.
- Model more and speak less. All students get fatigued by listening to someone talk for more than a few minutes. Physically show where papers are to be placed, demonstrate how the flip chart will be cut, and walk around the room to show how stations are arranged.
- Chunk lessons into small pieces.
- Scaffold upward to help all learners meet rigorous targets. Keep expectations high for all learners.

BACKGROUND KNOWLEDGE, RELEVANCE, AND LEARNING

All learners benefit from personally connecting to content. Marzano (2004) declares prior knowledge to be the strongest indicator of how well students will latch on to new content. For English learners, it's especially urgent to know that content presented in a second language is relatable. In social studies, for example, if students are studying longitude and latitude, they can mark their birthplace on a world map. Number the markers and have students determine the exact locations of their classmates' places of birth. When studying types of economies or governments, include familiar examples. With math word problems, include airports from students' home cities, popular sports from different regions of the world, and their city's architecture with angles or 3D shapes. In science, incorporate pictures of animals or flora from their region. Consider literature choices that tap into students' interests and backgrounds. Helping students feel like they belong at school is an ongoing process, beyond hanging flags of the world up in the cafeteria—although that's nice, too.

At one of the schools in which I taught, our population had experienced an increase in English learners. On a class trip to the media center, I observed that some of my students neglected to check out any books at all—the media center specialist noticed as well. She took a survey and ordered materials that were more interesting to our student population today, not a decade back. It is also useful to review the literature being read in classrooms. Do the selected readings have relevance for all learners? I had to address this issue when teaching a historical novel that included considerable colloquial language, such as *jest* for *just* and *shadder* for *shadow*. I recall looking at my students who were diligently trying to learn English and realized that this was not the best choice for every student. In math, examples that are relevant for other students might not connect with English learners. For example, students might not understand loss of yards in a football game, which I have used, due to two things: the terms *football* and *yards*. A simple solution is to use the football problem but also add another problem that includes the same kind of math, and allow students to select one of the two.

THE VOCABULARY JOURNEY

Understanding academic vocabulary is essential for every student's success. All students who receive direct vocabulary instruction tend to outperform groups without that instruction (Nagy & Townsend, 2012) and improve with strategies like graphic organizers and paired collaborations. Stahl and Fairbanks (1986) show that students at the 50th percentile who were instructed on the words they would encounter in a text scored as well on average as learners in the 83rd percentile.

The importance of vocabulary is well known, but so are the challenges. In a typical school day, new words come faster than students can make sense of them. Ten in science, a dozen in math, 15 in language arts, and in social studies, 20. Therefore, for truly effective vocabulary instruction, it's important to make good decisions about which words are the most essential for students to know. Editing the list to a manageable size is important for the most fundamental reason that students must have multiple exposures over time to learn new words. In addition, students require different types of meaningful exposures and opportunities to use and own the words (Stahl & Fairbanks, 1986; Nagy & Townsend, 2012). Simply putting words on the wall or giving students lists does not work. Students need time to practice, play with, and incorporate these words. Therefore, too many words may result in inadequate vocabulary development.

For English learners and other students as well, making vocabulary visual pays dividends in understanding and retention. According to Powell (1980), students can benefit significantly from imagery-associated words. Both meaning and recall are significantly enhanced with imagery over rote memorization or creating sentences. For English learners, it is especially important to have visuals rather than simply text.

To provide ample experiences with vocabulary, make every day vocabulary day. Vocabulary instruction is a commitment and requires a plan of action with multiple, engaging opportunities. Learners need to see, hear, draw, handle, and discuss vocabulary words. Vocabulary development, as I discuss in one of my earlier books (Rollins, 2014), is a journey over time in which proficiency develops gradually with multiple, varied exposures. Deepening understanding comes with practice. Therefore, when planning learning experiences, consider what this ongoing development will look like.

A SAMPLE VOCABULARY PLAN

In my work, I encourage educators to add important new words to the class TIP (Term-Info-Picture) anchor chart with great fanfare. They can consider adding an optional fourth column where English learners may add the word in their heritage language. So, if *obtuse* and *acute* are the two new words for the day, they are discussed and added to the anchor chart, and a picture is drawn. Many teachers find it helpful for students to generate their own charts and pictures in notebooks or with their devices. The next day, if a new critical word is introduced, that is added to the TIP. This is unlike word walls or premade lists with an overwhelming number of words. TIP charts provide ready-made access to words, so that if the teacher says *perpendicular* in class, help is a head-turn away.

The TIP chart, however, is just the anchor. Mastering vocabulary takes practice, and what that practice looks like depends on students' current levels of understanding. For example, on the day a new word is introduced, word art might be a perfect fit. This simple, creative technique asks that students take a word and craft it into a piece of art. For example, the word *plateau* might be written in the shape of a plateau. Similarly, a student might sketch the word *perimeter* in the shape of a fence. In language arts, a student might interpret the word *hyperbole* in all caps to show exaggeration: HYPERBOLE!

On the next day of our vocabulary journey, a new word or two will appear on the TIP. However, we cannot neglect the words from prior days,

Linear and Exponential Functions

T	**I**	**P**
TERM	INFORMATION	PICTURE f(x)
Continuous function	Change Occurs "gradually"	*[graph of increasing line]*
Discrete function	Change occurs "All AT ONCE"	*[graph with discrete points]*
Linear function	increases/decreases by "Equal" differences over "equal Intervals" "Constant Rate of Change"	*[two x/y tables]*
Exponential Function	increases/decreases by a "constant factor" "Common Ratio" r "variable Rate of change"	*[two x/y tables]*

Figure 2.1: BLAKE BOURG'S ALGEBRA I TIP CHART
Source: Armuchee High School, Floyd County

or students will not get the multiple exposures required to create meaning. Students can compare and contrast two of their words on a graphic organizer or create memory devices for the words. Songs can be made from the words—or students may applaud every time the words are used. Or just have students stand up and act out the words. Again, multiple exposures in varying ways deepen vocabulary understanding.

Since there are now more words on the list, your practice could include a word sort or Word Detective. Groups of students are provided cards with vocabulary words. Display a passage in which key vocabulary words have been removed. Student pairs can collaborate to decide where their word fits into the passage and attach it to the text on the screen. For example:

Two rays that share a common endpoint is called an _____. There are 360 degrees inside a _____. A _____ angle measures exactly 90 degrees.

An _____ angle measures less than 90 degrees. A _____ angle measure more than 90 degrees and less than 180 degrees. _____ is the distance measured around the outside of an object.

Word Bank: acute, obtuse, perimeter, right, angle, circle

A favorite game that I model with teachers is as simple as it is fun. As the vocabulary list builds, on a cube, write a new word on each side. On a second cube, write innovative things to do with the vocabulary word. For example, the first cube might include the words legislative, executive, judicial, impeach, veto, and cabinet. The second cube is where the action lies, with directions such as "Explain it in a pirate voice," "Explain it in a French accent," or "Talk only with your hands." At an optimum point in class, have two students roll the cubes in the middle of the room. "Turn to your partner and explain the legislative branch in a French accent!"

Vocabulary integration can be as simple as having students turn to a partner and share everything they know about two of their words. Other options include creatively mapping words out on graphic organizers. Students can also create bumper stickers or write them in circles, other shapes, or upside down, or make hats out of them—whatever works!

As the unit progresses, the sheer volume of words can create some confusion. Consider having students create videos of themselves talking or interviewing each other about their favorite vocabulary words. If they are shy about being on camera, students can draw faces on their fingers and let them star in the show. Vocabulary scavenger hunts can be fun as the class searches for real-world examples of academic vocabulary. Take a walk around the campus and find samples of perimeter, area, triangles, or circumference—compare them, talk about how to measure and classify them!

Vocabulary instruction is deliberate, ongoing, varied, and explicit. But it can also be novel and innovative. In Mr. Bourg's algebra class, whose TIP chart is pictured earlier, students actually drew the axis of symmetry directly on his face. This teacher worked that look all day in the hallways of the school. Every student will remember that critical term.

Compare this vocabulary journey with static lists on walls. What works in vocabulary instruction: multiple exposures over time in a variety of ways, imagery, easily understood definitions, conversations, games, and practice. And while these vocabulary strategies work for all learners, consider the impact on those learning a second language. Things English speakers might take for granted, like figuring words out from context clues in a passage, are more challenging for students who are missing vocabulary pieces.

SCAFFOLDING FOR ENGLISH LANGUAGE LEARNERS

Chapter One introduced scaffolding for ADHD learners, which removes barriers to learning new information by compensating for their deficits in working memory, organization, and structure. Scaffolds can take the form of bookmarks, foldables, mnemonics, sticky note reminders, computer apps, folder systems, or a host of other devices.

English language learners require scaffolding as well. And like our ADHD learners, the amount and nature of scaffolding will vary for individual students. Scaffolding can also support emerging readers. A simple example is the use of understandable synonyms. For example, if the posted learning target includes the word *determine*, jot down "find out" next to the word. In the math classroom, next to the word *product* write a simple math problem and circle the product in a bright color. You can do this on slides during the lesson, with simple synonyms or pictures for key words. In addition, consider annotating the text to be read that day in class to support ELL readers.

Premade language scaffolding devices can enable students to learn more and gain confidence. Bookmarks or foldables on comma rules, critical science terms, prefixes and suffixes, parts of speech, capitalization, and the difference in proper and common nouns are all examples. These can also be digitally created or pasted into an interactive notebook format that students can utilize for homework. Again, these supports will benefit other students as well. Having said that, scaffolding is a judicious process. These supports are pushed in as needed and faded as warranted by progress. For example, a paragraph might be partially constructed for a student. On a subsequent writing assignment, less material will be constructed. Ongoing practice with bilingual glossaries is a common scaffolding technique for English learners. Word problems in math might require annotating terms that denote which operations students will need, or numbered steps for support.

Any learner may need support to develop requisite skills. Ongoing observations and soft, ungraded formative assessments serve to guide decisions on scaffolding. Does the student have a language gap, a skills gap, or both?

In any new lesson that is heavy on academic vocabulary, consider providing students with video links in their heritage language prior to class. This will support students in gaining knowledge in their heritage language first. I have observed in classrooms that videos on phones or tablets give students the power to rewatch critical parts over and over. Using a device to get what they need right now without having to ask the teacher for help might be a tool worth incorporating.

TEXT SUPPORTS

Prior to reading, preview the text through the lens of critical vocabulary that is the most important to understanding the passage. Write and say these words to provide initial exposure. A safe, tactile strategy that I use is a prereading vocabulary sort. For example, I write nine words on pieces of paper and place them in bags. In groups, students place these words in three piles: Know It, Think I've Seen It, and Brand New. In whole group, we discuss the words and identify those that will be a primary focus. Or you can simply use sticky flags or other mechanisms (digital text often has tools for this) to highlight key words prior to reading. Say these key words together and write them on the board with simple synonyms.

As with all reading, students need to be aware of the clear purpose of reading a text. During reading, strategies should be employed such as annotating the text, highlighting the three most important parts of the text, or flow charting the sequence of events. These visual strategies enable teachers to respond to students' thoughts and to see their progress. Shortening text length is often appropriate and can be done by simply starring the most important passages students are to read.

Paired readings work well, so that as one student reads aloud, the partner takes notes on stickies and attaches them to the page. These notes are focused on the purpose of the reading, such as how characters change, use of figurative language, steps in a process, or causes of a war. After a few paragraphs, the students switch roles. When reading is complete, students pull off the sticky notes and organize their thoughts for a written or oral summary. Paired readings can also be silent. After establishing the purpose in reading, partners read a page silently and annotate their text. After a page, partners compare notes about the reading. Paired readings are structured, with each reader having a distinct job to do. After the text is read, students demonstrate what they have learned. This sharing might include a comparison of two characters, a quick write, an opinion, one change they would make, a sketch, or even a different ending. (Quick writes are just that—short opportunities to respond in written form. These are typically not graded, but frequently shared. The focus is on crafting ideas, rather than grammar or spelling.)

Getting all students to share ideas about their reading is a challenge. Often, the same few hands pop up. Conversation cubes encourage increased participation of all students, while scaffolding language. Create cubes with starters, such as "My favorite character," "I disagree with," or "I was surprised by." In groups, students roll a cube and complete the thought. In social studies, the cubes might have the simple words: who, what, when, where, and why. Two cubes enhance the fun and increase thinking. For example, create one cube that lists biomes, such as tundra and desert. For the second cube, rolled at the same time, include items like "characteristics," "location," and "describe in one word." Students take turns rolling cubes in their group, refer to their readings and notes, and respond to the cubes. Cubes provide students with opportunities to share what they know while practicing their new language.

Learning stations can be effective in differentiating content for English learners. A short video, varying levels of text, slides with pictures, manipulatives or labs, quick writes, games, drawing—stations enable students to hear, see, write, share, and touch a topic in different ways. Plus, stations provide teachers opportunities to work with a small group of students on reading, math, or vocabulary proficiency, so that emerging English learners do not have to respond in front of the entire group. Students should have a graphic organizer or note-taking device to jot down ideas as they move through stations. In addition, writing can be scaffolded by providing partially completed paragraphs or essays. For example, the teacher might provide the topic and closing sentences—students add three details in the middle. Stations also provide an effective structure for the ESL teacher to push in supports. Pushing in supports, rather than pulling students from class, allows all learners to be included.

The ESL or general education teacher might situate themselves in this station for targeted work.

And while there is an understandable need to implement teaching strategies to develop their new language, diligence is needed to see and develop the talents of these learners. Watch for opportunities for them to share their strengths. If students are creating a brochure, for example, one might be the artist, another the layout expert, and yet another the researcher.

INCREASING STUDENT AND PARENT INVOLVEMENT IN SCHOOL

Imagine how difficult it must be for a parent who does not speak the language of educators or understand the culture of the school to participate in a school meeting or event. Conversations about standardized scores, schedules, rules, academic progress, class placement, and extracurricular events may be overwhelming. Their children—who are themselves in the midst of learning the new language—often serve as unofficial translators.

In general, parents with more formal education tend to be more involved than others. For example, according to a report by Child Trends (2013), 87% of parents with a bachelor's degree or higher attended a school event, as compared to 54% of parents who did not complete high school. For parents volunteering or serving on a school committee, the gap is larger, with just 25% of those without diplomas serving, as compared to 65% of professional parents. Parents in poverty are less involved at school, with just 27% volunteering. Part of the reason, the study purports, is that lower-wage workers tend to have more rigid work schedules, so that it's more challenging to be available during school hours. In addition, parents who do not speak English have lower participation rates in schools. They may be understandably hesitant and nervous about coming to school. Will teachers and staff be welcoming? Will there be translators?

A study by Quiocho and Daoud (2006) questions some of the myths surrounding the perceptions of Latino parents' involvement in their children's education. When they queried teachers about school involvement, the responses revealed teacher frustrations with inadequate parental help with homework and concern that the parents were not participating at the school. However, the Latino parents expressed the need for workshops to support them in understanding how to help their children with school-work, a need for better communication between school and home, and an appreciation of personal phone calls inviting them to school. In addition, their perception was that non-Spanish speakers were given greater access to core curriculum, such as science and social studies.

As reported by Hiefield (2018), educators at an Oregon school real-ized that their use of largely digital methods was less effective in reach-ing Latino parents than others. Fewer of them had email accounts, or the accounts were going unchecked. So they established monthly tech-nology events in which parents set up online accounts and engaged in hands-on practice accessing their child's records. In addition, they spent time navigating the district's website, including the Spanish ver-sion. Babysitting and refreshments were provided, as well as additional translators.

Barriers that can keep parents from being more involved in school include events held during working hours, the high poverty rate among Hispanic families, materials sent home in English, and few school staff members who speak Spanish (Morton, 1992). Some families also believe that they are either ill prepared or lack the standing to question the school system. In addition, Morton advises that impersonal methods, such as flyers, are less effective than more personal touches. Face-to-face invita-tions, such as home visits, work well to build trust in the community, as well as the recognition that the Latino culture includes extended families, beyond the American nuclear model. Off-site social events in places where parents are comfortable are often more successful. In addition, it's advised to begin the program with parents' concerns—what's on their minds—as opposed to strictly the school's agenda.

Building connections with home cannot be the sole domain of ESL teachers (Brooks, Adams, & Morita-Mullaney, 2010). In some schools, the staff may view English learners as the primary responsibility of the ESL program. Assigning the bulk of phone calls home regarding content or behavior to ESL teachers or making them the sole bridge builders for extracurricular activities can limit the capacity of the students. These are everyone's students, and a narrow approach can stymie relationships between content teachers, leaders, and students.

RESEARCH TO PRACTICE

Learning all the academic content required in school is tough in any language. Mastering a new language while simultaneously latching on to new academic content—from math to biology to poetry—presents innumerable challenges to a child. From low graduation rates to lower scores on standardized tests to lack of preparation for college, this group of students is indeed vulnerable to underachievement and, as a whole, is not reaching their potential. School are searching for instructional models that better serve English learners, from fewer pullouts to dual immersion programs. Placing them in a classroom with no instructional modifications, however, is not our instructional best. For the general education teacher, faced with full classrooms and quick pacing guides, the good news is that there are easily implementable strategies that support language development while teaching content. Language scaffolding, such as chunking content, speaking more deliberately, increasing modeling, and incorporating visuals, tend to benefit all learners. A bigger challenge, perhaps, is peering through the language deficits to see the academic strengths of ELLs. In addition, conversations that tackle expectations might be in order: What do we expect from our English learners? Is it simply to make it through high school—or do we need to aim higher?

A good first start is perhaps getting to know these students and their families better. Some are refugees; others may have parents who work at the local university. There is a continuum of language proficiency in these students as well, both in their home language and in the second one. Their ability to converse at the lunchroom table may provide false impressions about their abilities to understand academic content and vocabulary, which is on quite another level. In addition, consider the role of ESL teachers, educators with specialized expertise. While they are important in facilitating conversations between parents, teachers, and leaders, they are sometimes left to be the sole contact with ELL parents. To maximize academic progress, parents also need direct access to content teachers and administrators.

In large measure, success for English language learners relies on replacing barriers with ongoing supports to access content and build language skills. In the midst of supporting them in content acquisition, we need to, as well, discover and accentuate their strengths and gifts. As demonstrated by current results, simply teaching content without modifying instruction is not a viable route.

QUESTIONS TO PONDER

- What is the graduation rate in your school or district for ELLs?
- What are the academic expectations for ELLs in your school?
- How successful are your school's programs to engage parents and extended families of ELLs?
- What steps can educators take to see a content lesson through the lens of ELLs?
- Is your instructional model for ELLs working?
- What steps can be taken to support English learners in becoming college ready?
- What attitudes exist regarding English learners in your building?
- What is your comfort level in building relationships with parents of English learners?

MOVING FORWARD

➤ What is your school's vision for ELLs? Is it high school graduation, or beyond? Are ELLs being providing avenues for advanced work? Are connections to home successful? If not, explore avenues to glean more involvement from ELL parents. _____

_____

_____

_____

_____

CHAPTER 3

Readers in Peril

The classroom is ready. The bulletin boards pop with color, and name placards are in place. Hope, excitement, and the smell of fresh pencils . . . the first day of kindergarten arrives. Children bravely let go of parents' hands, trusting their new teacher's assurance that it is indeed going to be a great day. Every teacher, parent, and leader want children to be successful at school. But before educators have even met them, forces have been in play that impact the most critical element of becoming well educated—reading. To say that a 5-year-old is already behind is upsetting—we want to believe that on the first day of school all children are beginning on the same start line. The reality is quite different. Some students enter school with decided disadvantages—they are positioned well behind the starting line, and others are already rounding the first turn. For these children (and every other reader) to reach their potential, a deliberate pre-K through 12 reading plan is essential.

A student's school journey to becoming a reader has three steps. First, students may acquire concepts that influence future reading skills before they even begin school. After they enter school, instructional methods used in lower grades can give them a great start. And third, fluency, reading comprehension, and vocabulary integration in all other grades support students in becoming skilled readers so that they can reach their academic potential.

THE STUDENTS WE'VE YET TO MEET

What parents and caretakers do to nurture reading readiness in preschoolers can significantly impact their future success. A longitudinal study including over 20,000 students and parents reports that students who enter kindergarten already recognizing letters, who have been read to at least three times per week, and who recognize shapes, numbers, and the concept of relative size have significantly higher reading skills in the spring of kindergarten and first grade (Denton & West, 2002). In addition, children who enter kindergarten already recognizing letters are more apt to score in the top 25th percentile in the spring of that year, compared to just 2% of children without that knowledge. This trend holds true in first grade as well, with 34% of the first group garnering top scores as opposed to just 5% of the group that arrived less prepared. They also score much higher in mathematics.

By the spring of kindergarten, students who began the year already recognizing letters are about twice as likely to understand letter-sound relationships at the beginning of words, and around three times as likely to do the same at the end of words than students who entered school without this knowledge. Students who entered school with these skills continue to have advantages in first grade in recognizing sight words, understanding words in context, and in math skills (Denton & West, 2002). Children who have been read to three times per week at home enter school with academic advantages.

A positive attitude about school also matters. Students who arrive at school with a positive approach to learning are more than two times as likely to score in the top 25% in reading and math in the spring of kindergarten and the first grade. In sum, children entering school that have been read to three times per week or more, who recognize letters, shapes, and numbers, and who understand the concept of relative size have significant advantages over students without these resources. In addition, soft skills are learned through frequent reading at home, such as paying attention, being persistent, and even how learning can be pleasurable (Denton & West, 2002).

What about students who are read to on a daily basis prior to entering school? Kalb and van Ours (2013) show that students who are read to six to seven times per week enter school in effect 12 months ahead of students without those experiences. Literacy and numeracy benefits from daily reading, according to this research, extend long term, at least through the ages of 10 or 11. Interestingly, the parents' educational attainment level had little impact for new kindergarteners who were read to frequently—their skills improved about the same amount as those with parents who had higher educational levels. Children who were read to three to five days per week entered school with about a six-month increase. There is a clear association with reading frequently to preschool children and increased early reading scores, vocabulary development, and mathematics. Talk about a head start.

In addition, evidence exists that preschoolers who learned about sounds in words have advantages. Dr. Sally Shaywitz (2003) summarizes research involving preschoolers who practiced categorizing words according to beginning, middle, or ending sounds. For example, children sorted pictures with similar beginning sounds, such as *hat* and *hen*, and ending sounds, like *bed* and *lad*. A second group of preschoolers engaged in a general language experience. The group with the focus on sounds showed a significant improvement in later reading and spelling. This demonstrates the importance of reading experiences prior to entering kindergarten.

And then there's the vocabulary gap among children entering school. Hart and Risley's (1995) groundbreaking—and heartbreaking—findings reveal a significant divide in vocabulary skills along economic lines. Three-year-olds from families on welfare often possess about 70% of the vocabulary of children from working-class homes. The gap, however, between economically disadvantaged students and children from homes of professional and middle-class families is much wider. The poorer children only knew about 45% of the vocabulary used in that group. The nature of talk at home also differed along economic lines. More affluent parents used a richer, more varied vocabulary with their children. In addition, these parents routinely asked their children more questions and provided more positive feedback to them. Because of the correlation between vocabulary and reading, the limited vocabulary of poorer students matters. In addition, as school progresses, vocabulary with academic content increases. For students who are lacking incidental vocabulary, often learned at home, the text can become daunting, as new academic vocabulary merges with other unfamiliar words—which other children came to school already knowing.

Students who arrive ready to read have a decided advantage. And while most children entering kindergarten will learn these skills in school, students who arrive on day one ready to read hit the ground running—and keep moving. Armed with this information, what measures can be employed to inform parents, pediatricians, preschools, and day care centers to lay the groundwork for better readers before educators even meet them? About 67% of new kindergarteners recognize letters and just 31% understand beginning letter-sound relationships (Denton & West, 2002). What initiatives can be spawned to improve those numbers?

COMMUNITY INITIATIVES TO INCREASE READING AT HOME

A school initiative to enhance early literacy could include partnering with the local public library. Consider inviting library representatives to attend school events to share information, facilitate library card registrations, and develop rapport with families. Ask them to have a story-time session at the school for younger siblings during a parent night or to display samples of books available. Explore ways to bring the library to families, especially during the summer. Transportation is often an issue for lower-income families; some libraries provide resources through a bookmobile.

Health departments, pediatricians, preschools, and day care centers in the community routinely interface with parents of preschoolers. "Are you reading to your child every day?" is a question pediatricians would surely add to their wellness checkups. Local schools could facilitate conversations between school media specialists, public librarians, day care workers, and preschools about the kinds of books that support early reading. And in our own buildings, teachers could assign older students to read to younger siblings at home. In addition, parent organizations might organize book drives to get books to those who can't afford to buy them.

Abundant research connects students' reading experiences at home and subsequent success at school (Denton & West, 2001; Kalb & van Ours, 2013). Reading can be an academic equalizer. Reading at home can also instill the pleasure of learning something new, of beginning to understand the code of letters and sounds, of language development and vocabulary, and even sharing a wonderful story with a family member. Reading at home sparks conversations with more diverse vocabulary words. Books provide a launching pad for ideas, illustrations, and possibilities. Those of us who love to read cannot fathom a world without this skill. And, with all the inequalities in this world, a library card will (hopefully) always be free—transportation, unfortunately, is not.

WHAT HAVE WE DONE?

In an April 2019 PBS news feature, one mother tearfully details how her dyslexic son would claim to be sick or even hide rather than attend school (Stark, 2019). Another parent talks about frustration with schools who were supposed to have all the reading answers. And yet another shares the psychological trauma her child has endured from not being able to figure out reading. An elementary teacher bravely admits that she was never taught in college how to teach reading. She explains that she had been giving students sight words and the sounds letters make and "hoping they put it all together." A leader at the Arkansas Department of Education worries about the impact of past generations of not teaching students explicitly how to read with a science-based approach—research that's been available for decades now. She ponders, "What have we done?" The school principal, whose own son has reading difficulties, explains that her journey with her own child has opened her eyes to leading a school down a better reading path. (This video is available online.)

In this video, children share their views on reading. An elementary girl explains her simple hope: that she will be able to see a word, know it, and just keep reading. A boy talks about how great it would be to read a chapter book and not get tripped up by the big words. The state of Arkansas is on a new hopeful path to better reading, with a cornerstone of teacher training rooted in science. Other states are on similar paths, led largely by parents with dyslexic children. This 8-minute video demonstrates the perspectives of stakeholders about the reading problem. In addition, the feature wonderfully demonstrates what reading instruction looks like now in these schools' lower grades. Overarching questions emerge: What reading methods should be employed to create proficient readers? What does science tell us about teaching a child to read?

What these parents and teachers may not realize is that a war has been going on for many years. And while no shots have been fired, the casualties have mounted, particularly the countless number of children whose lives were forever altered by missing critical pieces of reading instruction. The reading wars developed a battlefield with two sides. Simply put, one group favored a systematic phonemic awareness and phonics-based approach. This approach focuses on teaching how sounds turn into words, of mastering the code of reading. The other approach, whole language, puts literature at the center but without explicit devices to make sense of sounds, letters, and the formation of words. And while no one questions the importance of exploring captivating literature, this approach largely relies upon students guessing at words. Elementary educators who teach multiple subjects every day with very little planning time have been caught in the middle of the philosophical war over how to teach reading, a skill that will impact a child's entire life. The teacher's honest comments speak volumes: How many educators are simply left to their own devices to discover the best ways to teach reading? Parents of children with reading difficulties are making serious headway in ending the reading wars—with the goal of using scientifically proven methods that explicitly teach every child to read, as well as ramping up early assessment of reading problems.

UNLOCKING THE READING CODE

Dr. Sally Shaywitz (2003) is a professor of Pediatrics at Yale University and an expert in reading and dyslexia. She explains that reading is hardly a natural process, but rather a human invention. She calls reading the converse of speaking, because a reader must convert printed words to sounds. The abstract symbols on a page that form words consist of phonemes representing sounds, the smallest units of speech, which are essentially building blocks of written and spoken words. Forty-four phonemes are used to create every word in the English language. To make this conversion from print to sound, words must first be broken down into phonemes for processing by the language system.

A process called the phonological model takes a child from simply seeing symbols to understanding the formation of words to the realization that letters stand for the sounds the child hears when that word is spoken. This process follows a logical sequence. A child realizes first that words consist of smaller segments, and next that these segments correspond to sounds. Written letters now become linked to spoken language. The realization that letters on the printed page match with the same phonemes as when the word is spoken begins to sink in. The relationship between written and spoken words solidifies—both can be broken down into sounds, and the symbols on the page represent sounds. This connection is known as the alphabetic principle, which must be mastered by children in order to learn to read. Shaywitz (2003) explains that speaking, unlike reading, is a natural process for humans. Readers have to make the leap of translating symbols into speech, something our brains know how to do—otherwise, letters will remain meaningless symbols on a page. Teaching a child to read is a process that systematically unlocks this code.

WHAT WORKS IN READING INSTRUCTION?

Over 20 years ago, at the behest of the United States Congress, a group of top experts in reading was convened to exhaustively research the most effective, scientifically proven approaches to teaching children to read. This research was to be communicated quickly and effectively to educators. This National Reading Panel consisted of leading scientists, reading teachers, college of education faculty members, and parents. (Dr. Shaywitz was a member.) Their exhaustive work took three years and resulted in a 500-page document, available online for everyone to absorb (National Reading Panel, 2000). And while reading research continues, this panel's work has answered many of questions about the best path for teaching reading. Its thorough and pragmatic report does not recommend which resources or programs to purchase but outlines research so that schools can match potential resources to the evidence available.

This report should have brought an end to the reading wars, or at least an armistice. The summary below gives some of their key findings about effective instruction. Their report is organized by these components of teaching reading: alphabetics, which includes phonemic awareness and systematic phonics instruction, fluency, and reading text, which includes vocabulary development and comprehension. And while the alphabetics components are a stronger focus in lower grades, all educators in all grades share responsibility for fluency and reading comprehension. According to the National Assessment of Educational Progress, in 2017 just 36% of eighth grade readers scored at or above proficiency in reading;

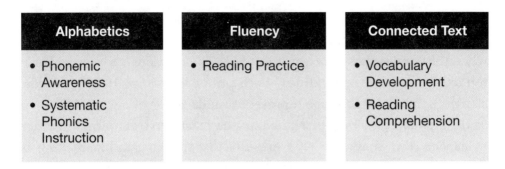

Figure 3.1: THE FIVE COMPONENTS OF TEACHING READING
Source: Adapted from National Reading Panel (2000)

fourth grade came in at 37%—so 64% of eighth graders and 63% of fourth graders scored below proficient (NAEP, 2017).

Figure 3.1 summarizes the five components of teaching reading. A sampling of strategies that mirror the research from the panel follows.

Alphabetics: Phonemic Awareness

Phonemic awareness is the ability to understand how sounds in spoken language make words. For example, the word *me* has two sounds, or phonemes; *toe* also has two phonemes, but three letters. Phonemic awareness instruction teaches students to discern and manipulate the sounds of spoken words. This is different than phonics instruction, which teaches the relationship between sounds and letters, which facilitates the reading and spelling of written words. Before students are able to read print, they must first understand how sounds work. Phonemic awareness is typically a weak area for struggling readers. When children begin school, according to the National Reading Panel, the two key predictors for how they will fare in reading for their first two critical years are phonemic awareness and letter recognition. Tasks in teaching phonemic awareness typically include: (a) phoneme isolation, such as recognizing sounds in words; (b) phoneme identity, or recognizing common sounds in different words; (c) phoneme categorization, such as identifying words that don't belong; (d) phoneme blending, such as listening to a sequence of sounds and combining them; (e) phoneme segmentation, such as breaking a word into sounds by tapping out; and (f) phoneme deletion, such as identifying a word after a phoneme has been removed. Some of the key findings from the meta-analysis from the National Reading Panel (2000) about explicitly teaching phonemic awareness include:

- Reading significantly improved in classrooms teaching phonemic awareness compared to classrooms without it. Reading improvements spanned grade levels across a variety of teaching conditions and students.
- Children of varying abilities improved their reading with phonemic awareness instruction, and the effects were lasting.
- Spelling improved, with the exception of disabled readers. (The panel noted spelling as an ongoing trouble spot for disabled readers.)
- The best results were in classrooms in which students were explicitly and systematically taught to manipulate phonemes with letters in small-group settings.

Alphabetics: Systematic Phonics Instruction

Phonics instruction teaches readers the relationship between sounds and letters and how to apply this information to reading and spelling. According to the National Reading Panel, systematic phonics instruction significantly benefits K–6 readers, including those with reading difficulties. The panel's report considers systematic phonics instruction critical in kindergarten and the lower grades and valuable for higher grades as well. Systematic instruction is different than an incidental approach, in which during the course of reading, for example, a word is examined. Especially encouraging are gains shown by low socioeconomic status (SES) students, low-achieving and disabled readers, some of our most vulnerable learners. Some of the key benefits to students in classrooms utilizing systematic phonics instruction:

- Kindergarteners showed improved reading and spelling, and first graders improved in reading comprehension, decoding, and spelling. Among older students, decoding, spelling, and oral reading improved.
- Disabled readers reaped significant improvements with systematic synthetic phonics instruction, including reading words and processing text. Importantly, low-SES students, low-achieving students, and

children with learning disabilities all improved. Low-SES students particularly improved in word reading and alphabetic knowledge.

- Across all grades, good readers became better spellers as a result of intensive phonics instruction. (Again, spelling issues remained for reading-disabled learners.)
- Educators should emphasize how students can apply their knowledge of phonics in their daily reading and writing.
- Some students will develop phonics understanding and application more readily. Educators should have an action plan for these students.
- Phonics skills are delivered within a reading framework that includes phonological awareness, fluency, and reading comprehension—it is not the entire reading plan.

Fluency

Fluency is the ability to read text accurately with speed and expression. The National Reading Panel considers fluency essential to reading comprehension, and views reading practice as essential to developing fluency. The panel determined that guided oral repeated reading, with guidance by teachers, parents, or peers, has significant positive effects, such as improved word recognition, reading comprehension, and fluency. Gains were realized across grade levels. The significantly positive impact was seen in regular and special education classrooms, both for good readers and those with reading difficulties.

Hundreds of studies, the panel notes, reveal that good readers read more; weak readers read less. The more students read, the better their comprehension, fluency, and vocabulary get. Independent silent reading is generally thought to increase reading achievement. But the panel was unable to find solid evidence that programs that encourage large amounts of silent reading with little teacher guidance produced positive results in achievement, including fluency. Further, independent silent reading is ineffective as the sole type of reading practice, especially for students who have not yet developed word reading and alphabetic skills.

Reading Text: Vocabulary Development and Reading Comprehension

Vocabulary development and reading comprehension go hand-in-hand in developing readers. Students who possess large, rich vocabularies find it easier to understand what is being read. Developing students' vocabularies can yield gains in reading comprehension. Understanding words, however, requires multiple exposures over time in different contexts. Effective vocabulary instruction highlighted by the panel included previewing vocabulary words prior to reading, multiple exposures in varying contexts, and utilizing different techniques, rather than doing only one thing. In addition, substituting simpler words for difficult ones especially supports lower readers.

Reading comprehension is an active process in which the reader interacts with the text. It can be improved by imbedding strategies that align with the research as follows:

- Comprehension improves when readers relate text to their own prior knowledge and experiences.
- Awareness of their own thought processes while reading improves comprehension.
- Cooperative learning can enhance comprehension.
- Construction of graphic organizers and mapping can support comprehension.
- Question generation and answering supports comprehension.
- Understanding story structure as a means of recalling the content of the story is effective.
- Summarizing in which readers integrate ideas and make generalizations from the text enhances comprehension.

WHY IS READING SO EASY FOR SOME...
AND SO DAUNTING FOR OTHERS?

According to Shaywitz (2003), 70–80% of children are successful in breaking the reading code—of converting written symbols into sounds. But that leaves behind a whole lot of students in the other 20–30%. In a school of 500, for example, 150 students might be in peril of reading failure. Students with dyslexia have a language system glitch that makes phonemic awareness, the essential element in reading, very difficult (Shaywitz, 2003, p. 52). Breaking the spoken word into underlying sounds is a distinct weakness, as is decoding. This roadblock in their language functions presents a barrier to decoding and identifying words. In addition, memorizing and retrieving words in a timely fashion are particularly challenging (Shaywitz, 2003). They might be very adept at listening to a story and recounting the key points and be very bright students with intellectual gifts but demonstrate significant hurdles in turning words in print into sounds. Dyslexia is by far the most common reading disorder under the umbrella category of learning disabilities. According to Mather and Wendling (2012), almost 80% of students served under special education are due to reading difficulties.

Technology today allows researchers to peer into students' brains while they are reading. Studies of these images from MRI's are leading researchers to new paths to help readers. One theory is that there are actually two groups of dyslexics, one of which is born with this glitch in brain systems, which can be viewed on the image. While struggling with reading, this group exhibits higher verbal abilities and compensatory skills. The other group, researchers surmise, lacks good reading instruction and/or a home environment supportive of building language. The wiring, researchers propose, is there, but not activated—and not working properly. But what's incredible about these studies is that images taken right after an effective reading intervention showed changes in the brain. These students looked more like good readers. And there's more! A year after the reading interventions, these improved readers' brains demonstrated evidence of repair—they looked like the brains of children who had always been good readers. This actual, visual evidence of the impact of reading interventions on new readers is a powerful testament to scientifically based reading instruction and solid teaching (Shaywitz, 2003).

Those interventions look a great deal like the National Reading Panel's meta-analysis. Students with dyslexia need the same elements in place to learn to read, but more of them, typically with additional small-group instruction.

Practice and feedback are critical elements in fluency. Guided oral repeated reading is a most effective practice technique, up to at least grade five, but for some students even in middle and high school. This oral reading in a safe setting provides the opportunity for students to apply what they have learned, get some practice on difficult words, and hear words pronounced correctly by the teacher, thus establishing a correct model of the word in the brain. After practicing with the teacher, students can reread the text with a peer (Shaywitz, 2003). Silent reading alone does not provide the needed feedback from an experienced reader, and fluency requires practice. Struggling readers, understandably, tend to avoid reading. Stronger readers jump in and read more. Less practice time for reluctant readers can accentuate the reading gap.

STRATEGIES THAT MIRROR THE RESEARCH

Vocabulary development is critical to reading comprehension. The numbers may vary, but students should know about 90–95% of the words in a text to be able to read it. Of course, students have different working vocabularies. Good practices for reading are similar to techniques that build language development in English learners:

1. Word sort previews: Create a simple word sort on cards of new or difficult vocabulary critical to understanding the text. As a confidence builder, include a couple of words that most students already know. For example, for a passage about the respiratory system, the tricky new words might include tonsils, tongue, lungs, breathe, and nasal passage—let's add mouth as a confidence builder. In whole or small groups, students sort in three piles: know it, seen it, or brand new. Practice saying the word correctly as a group and demonstrate the meaning of the words on the body. Now, as they read the text, students react as the words reveal themselves. If peer reading, they might use sticky flags. For an oral read, students can clap, raise hands, and so on as the words appear. After reading, revisit the sort: can they add more words to the "know it" pile?

2. Plastic sheets can be placed over text that shouldn't be written on. Preview the new words and circle them with wipe-off markers. As students uncover the words, they mark their text by placing a synonym or picture in the margins.

3. Pre-annotate passages for some students prior to reading, with easier synonyms of the tricky words.

4. Use TIP (term-info-picture) anchor charts (introduced in Chapter 2). As new vocabulary is introduced, write the word on the TIP chart. Talk about the word in easy-to-understand terms and create a classroom definition. Next, create a picture of the word. Pictures enhance

memory and understanding of words. Since vocabulary is learned over time with multiple exposures, the anchor chart provides an easy reference for words. For instance, if the word segregation is used in class, students unsure of the meaning can quickly glance at the TIP chart.

CONNECTING TO PRIOR KNOWLEDGE

Reading comprehension is heavily dependent upon students' prior knowledge. What the reader already knows connects to the text on the page. Even if every word is familiar, there can be a misfire without prior knowledge. For example, if the first sentence of a passage reads, "The bear market appears to be waning—the bulls are on the move. The rally ended with the Nasdaq up 3% for the week." Simple reading for someone who knows a little about the stock market—in fact, it's great news! But a reader without that knowledge could potentially read 95% of the words and think this is about live bulls and bears running amok. One reader is very glad to have an investment account; the other is wondering why bears were at the market in the first place. To understand this passage, readers must first know these key terms: a bear market means that stock prices are down; a bull market is positive; and the Nasdaq is an index of stocks. It's an acronym that, over time, stopped being capitalized. Now you're ready to read. Before reading a passage, support students in connecting to the text by tapping into—or even establishing—prior knowledge.

Strategies that use or create knowledge are as wide-ranging as the text students are preparing to read. For example, if you are about to read the novel *The Giver*, by Lois Lowry, you might have students keep a log of choices they've been allowed to make in their lives over the course of 24 hours. Or readers might debate the merits of these topics prior to reading:

- It's a good idea for community leaders to assign a career to me.
- Community leaders are the best ones to select marriage partners.
- My parents have the right to know all of my thoughts.
- Making decisions about my life is stressful.

If students will be reading about banking in their personal finance class, they can be presented with a real-world problem: "You just got your first job. You are officially on your own. You'll need to get a bank account for your first paycheck. Your task is to research banks in the area and decide which one best fits your needs. What are you looking for in a bank? Take this survey as a starting point in your quest for the best bank."

BANKING SURVEY

What kind of bank best fits your needs? Rank in importance from 1 to 5.

1. ___ I want easy access to ATMs.
2. ___ I plan on doing most of my banking online.
3. ___ I want to earn the most interest on my account(s).
4. ___ I don't want to pay a bunch of fees.
5. ___ I want people to know me when I walk into a branch.

In science, students might begin with a short lab or demonstration, such as examining items that are transparent, translucent, or opaque. In all subjects, readers can prepare by responding to pictures or short videos. "Jot down the differences you see in these pictures between invertebrates and vertebrates." Or "Look for similarities between Roman and Greek architectures." Active thinking is key here. Rather than simply watching videos or pictures flash by, students need to respond. If students are preparing to study the 1960s, what better way is there to get started than a series of pictures of 60s fashion, cars, technology, and political figures? Compare the 60s to what you see today.

Strategies that access prior knowledge not only increase comprehension but also clarify the purpose of reading. Students will be equipped to mark their text when they see banking characteristics they are seeking, ways a character's life is like theirs, or differences in types of rocks. They can flag their text, write in their margins, or star important items, giving the text more meaning and connectedness. These prereading strategies support students in engaging actively with the text.

Student-generated questions serve to get readers thinking about what they would like to know about the reading. They spark intellectual curiosity and embed purpose in reading. The following three strategies encourage more students to respond, rather than the same few students raising their hands.

GENERATING QUESTIONS BEFORE READING:
THREE EASY STRATEGIES

Question Sun

A question sun is a graphic organizer with a simple topic in the middle. The shape can be varied for novelty, but structures resembling a wheel, a sun, or stars work well. They provide a center with adjacent spaces for student questions. For example, if the class will be reading about thunderstorms today, that word goes in the middle. What do you want to know about storms? Students create questions—sticky notes work well for this—which get placed on the structure. As the class reads, some of the answers will be revealed. As they uncover the answers, students respond right on the figure. You can implement this first in whole group, and then students can learn to create them on their own.

Question Cubes

Question cubes add to student engagement by incorporating touch and a little mystery. On the sides of a cube (party favor boxes found online are very inexpensive and work well), write question starters, such as Why? How? What? These can increase in thinking level as the class progresses. Students take turns rolling the cube and creating questions they would like answered in the reading. Many of the answers will unfold as the reading progresses. Cubes can also be an effective addition to phonics instruction. One cube can have the beginnings of words, such as *bl*, *gr*, and *s*. The second cube can have the end, such as *and*. Students roll the two cubes and create words.

Question Cards

Question cards make a game of questioning. On index cards, write question cues or starters. In groups, students pass out a few cards to each player. Students select a card they want to play, placing it in the center. If the reading is about seasons, for example, one might ask, "What's the hottest place on earth?" Then next: "Why does it snow in the winter?" As they read, they discover answers to many of these questions.

What do these three questioning strategies have in common? They encourage every student to think about and pose questions about the

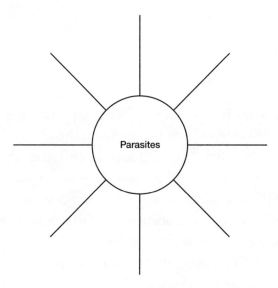

Figure 3.2: QUESTION SUN

upcoming reading. They are highly engaging—every student will roll a cube or play a card. Will the reading answer all of them? Probably not—but that's also a learning experience for students. We'll have to do more research on this, won't we?

DURING-READING STRATEGIES

Prereading strategies that connect to prior knowledge, generate questions, or provide deep thinking help readers establish a clear purpose for reading. For example, after looking at photos of the Gettysburg Cemetery, students will be more intellectually curious and will have context about the reading. Their purpose in reading may be to select three key points that Lincoln made in the Gettysburg Address that resonate with them. Students can flag these points, jot down ideas on the flags, and get ready to discuss their ideas with peers. If the purpose in reading is to compare and contrast two characters, they can use two different-colored highlighters, sticky notes, or a graphic organizer. If the purpose is to explain the causes of an event, students can simply code their text C for each cause. For a longer stretch of reading, students can utilize "highwriting," in which they highlight small pieces and then summarize in the margins. Or readers can simply annotate in their margins. These strategies support attentive, focused reading. The visible nature ensures that students are, in fact, reading, and prepare them to share what they have read, whether in writing or just verbally with a partner. Whether the content is science, health, or social studies, these three parts are in play:

1. Articulate the purpose of this reading: tap into (or construct) background knowledge or utilize questioning techniques to narrow in on it.
2. Embed during-reading strategies to track thinking, demonstrate connection to text, and identify purpose in reading. Examples might be annotating the text, highwriting, sticky notes, or graphic organizers.
3. Include a mechanism to tell about what students have read, which may just be talking to an elbow partner, doing a writing exercise, drawing, or other creative endeavor. (An example of an ineffective practice is simply to assign pages to read.)

DEVELOPING FLUENCY

Fluency is the ability to read accurately with speed and expression. Readers need a great deal of practice throughout school, not just in lower grades. Proficient, skilled readers tend to enjoy reading and read more often. Struggling readers, understandably, shy away from reading. This contributes to the Matthew Effect (Stanovich, 1986), in which weaker readers fall farther and farther behind, while stronger readers take off. (The phrase comes from "the rich get richer and the poor get poorer" from the Gospel of Matthew.) A technique proven to be not very effective is round-robin reading. Students don't read enough during these sessions to build fluency, often just a paragraph or two. Plus, it's a very disengaging approach. While one student is reading, all the others are passively awaiting their turn, and the cleverest readers will figure out that they can just sit idly until their turn. Popcorn reading, in which students read a segment and then select another reader to continue, is ineffective for building fluency. Students are often focused simply on when their turn might arise, and the choppy cadence diminishes fluency.

Guided oral reading is specifically mentioned by the National Reading Panel (2000) as integral to building fluency. This can be implemented in different ways, but typically a teacher first models fluent reading. Readers then read the text quietly for a bit, and then aloud, often with several rereads, while getting feedback from the teacher. Audiobooks also provide models of fluency—readers first listen and then practice passages. In one school in which I worked, students from higher grades paired with younger ones to model fluency and facilitate practice reading. Parents also play a key role in building fluency at home.

Whisper reading is a technique for small-group instruction in which all students read at the same time, but in a whisper. The teacher cues readers one at a time to increase the volume of their voice. This allows students to read more, but it's a safer learning situation than round robin, in which stress can build while awaiting your one big turn for a paragraph. Whisper reading gives teachers opportunities to provide feedback and students practice time for more text.

Paired readings are effective in all grades, if feedback structures are in place. As mentioned in Chapter 2, a good starting place is assigning the roles of reader and scribe. While one reads aloud, the partner jots down notes that align with the purpose of reading. With a silent reading, partners turn and discuss their notes at a designated point in the passage. As readers become more proficient, paired readings can be adapted. For example, older students can be provided with a map for reading a chapter. Student one is charged with certain responsibilities, such as detailing the traits of a particular character. Student two might tackle a different character. After reading a few pages, they compare notes and create a compare-and-contrast organizer for the two characters. Paired readings for older students can incorporate silent, oral, and choral reads. For portions heavy with dialogue, pairs can act out roles. What these paired reading structures have in common are that more text is being read, students give and receive feedback, and structures are in place. The presence of feedback and accountability to a partner can enhance fluency. An example of an ineffective practice would be just pulling two desks together to read.

Novel units pose particular challenges to building fluency. Because reading them is time consuming, there's a temptation to simply read large segments of the books to students. And while readers benefit from the modeling of a fluent reader, is the balance of who's doing the reading tipped too far toward the teacher side of the equation? In this scenario in which students passively sit and listen for long periods of time, student choice of not only what to read but how to read it may suffer. A shared literacy experience of books that we all love certainly has value.

The flip side, however, is that every student is reading the same book at the same level, often at the same pace. At the end of the day, have we moved all readers upward? Are they becoming more fluent? Was this particular novel critical to the education of all children, or would literature circles have been a better fit? These are big decisions teachers make in classrooms every day to increase the fluency of all students. My personal rule of thumb is that if every student will be reading the same book chosen for them, choices need to be woven into the work they do. For example, do you want to read today with a partner, on your own, or in the teacher circle? Would you like to mark your text with sticky flag notes, highlighting key points, or a graphic organizer? Would you like to summarize your reading by taping a video, writing an online review, or creating an illustration?

A particular challenge in secondary grades is the depth and pace of the content. When planning lessons, there might be a temptation for teachers to go home, do all the reading required, and organize the information gleaned into a slideshow presentation. In that scenario, teachers make all of the important decisions about the reading. In effect, the teacher has completed all three parts of a reading lesson: establishing purpose, documenting thinking, and acting on what was read. The teacher has decided what was important, organized what was learned, and created a product. The students will be the passive recipients of that information. Careful decisions should be made every day about what the teacher needs to explain and demonstrate, and what students can explore on their own. To develop readers, they must read more.

MOTIVATING STUDENTS TO PRACTICE READING

Being a struggling reader can feel pretty awful. Is reading aloud in front of classmates worth the risk of embarrassment or, worse, shame? Withdrawing from the task of reading is understandable and largely self-protective—reading should never hurt, but sometimes it does. To get better, however, involves practice. How do we continue improvement in reading with a group that is reluctant to read? In an interesting study by Guthrie et al. (2004), the researchers merged effective reading strategies, such as connecting to prior knowledge and questioning techniques, with motivational strategies. Techniques such as hands-on strategies, choices in reading, using interesting text, content goals, and collaborative reading were incorporated. Students chose things like which animal they wanted to study and the informational text they wanted to read to gather that information. Teachers guided students in choosing text that was appropriate in difficulty and suited for their topic. Students joined teams with similar interests and text choices and were given ample opportunities to share information and questions about their readings. This science setting might include a hands-on lab experience. These third grade students were provided with interesting, colorful texts from which to choose for their work. In addition, reading strategies were modeled and taught, such as questioning, tapping into prior knowledge, and summarizing. In one group, students were taught strategies without the motivational piece; the other group had both. The results are important, although not surprising. The students with both features of teaching reading strategies combined with motivational techniques scored higher on reading comprehension and were more strategic readers. In addition, teachers and students both reported an increase in motivation.

In sum, teaching reading strategies is not enough. There has to be something more for readers, especially those who struggle, to want to genuinely engage. Interesting text, choices, and opportunities to collaborate and share work engage readers. The good news from this study is that when these kinds of measures improve motivation, students more readily use the strategies they have been taught. With text that lacks relevance, interest, or choice, why bother?

Educators often think of reading in two parts: learning to read in lower grades, and reading to learn from around third grade forward. True. But this does not mean, however, that older students can simply be handed a chemistry book and be expected to jump right in and read to learn. While lower-grade teachers do a lot of the heavy lifting in reading, all educators share in creating proficient readers. Students must continually improve in reading. It is often said that every teacher is a reading teacher, because in all content classes, students are called upon to navigate difficult text with challenging vocabulary.

Station teaching is an instructional avenue mentioned already for both ADHD and English learners. For the ADHD learner, stations provide movement, chunking, and novelty. For ELLs, the benefits include chunking, vocabulary opportunities, and differentiated experiences. Stations are also useful for encouraging more reading by all students without feeling overwhelmed. In reading stations, students read a portion of text and engage in a meaningful task at each location. Then they move. The brain gets a break and resets attention. The combination of movement and chunking supports student engagement. Another compelling feature of reading stations is the ability to differentiate for reading levels. There might be articles of varying difficulty, and some might include more illustrations. Important paragraphs can be starred, so that a slower reader can hit the high spots. (High readers can be provided with advanced passages during this time.)

In addition, annotation of unfamiliar vocabulary is helpful. For example, the word *ubiquitous* might have a note that says "everywhere." Video segments are helpful to provide a summary of the learning target—providing a different learning channel for weaker readers. If students are studying the Cold War, for example, each spot could feature a different leader. In science, stations might detail elements of the water cycle. With six diverse stations with short reads, content reading is more manageable—and motivational—than sitting and reading a very long piece of text. A simple graphic organizer to record notes from the stations is a good accompaniment. Students can also work in pairs for further support. In addition, hands-on opportunities can be incorporated as well, such as map skills, labs, or vocabulary sorts. After working in stations, students return to groups to discuss what they have learned. Reading stations can inspire more reading in different ways to build fluency in content reading. Rather than handing students a dozen pages to read, this approach facilitates a large amount of reading but is more engaging.

A different approach that has the impact of stations without moving students is utilizing placemats. Situate students in groups of four. Create a structure from chart paper that has four equal parts, with a circle in the middle. Each student will have a distinct job to do with the same or different text. First, students work on their own and research their topic. Second, students teach each other what they have learned. Third, the group creates a common task that is described in the circle in the middle. For example, if the text is about the challenges of moving to a different

Figure 3.3: PLACEMAT READING
Source: Ashley Bridges, Greensboro Elementary School, Greene County

country, each reader takes a different perspective: for example, costs, employment, legal requirements, and cultural barriers. After sharing, students create a task for the middle, such as the pros and cons of moving. If the text is about planets, students choose one of four planets to study. After reading about their planet, they share and then create the center task, such as a chart on the four planets. In language arts, students might select a character to study first, and then create a compare-and-contrast diagram in the center. In all of these situations, students' sections should be covered with notes as they read. Stations, paired readings, literature circles, and placemats are strategies that move more of the reading onto students' shoulders.

In the placemat example in Figure 3.3, Ms. Bridges's students read the same text on the practice of allowing students to skip grade levels, but each reader was tasked with defending different positions on the subject. For example, one student took notes on the principal's perspective. In the center, students collaborate to decide whether it is beneficial for students to skip grades.

THE TOLL IT TAKES

Imagine going to school for seven hours a day and not being good at it—dreading being called upon to simply read. It can take a toll on a child, and even make them feel sad, lonely, angry, unpopular. Morgan, Farkas, and Wu (2012) found that fifth graders who were weak readers used these words to describe themselves more frequently than stronger readers. Being a weak reader can spiral into unproductive behaviors, such as withdrawing from tasks, frustration in class, and anxiety. At school and home, this can result in incomplete tasks, reluctance to practice reading, and negativity toward reading.

Or worse. Poor reading ability can develop into aggression or acting out at school. Anxiety and depression are increased in this vulnerable group. For older students, there are even reports of increased suicide rates. Not being able to keep up with peers and falling short of academic expectations of teachers and parents can spur withdrawal, isolation, and worse at school. Reading is at the center of children's educational expectations every school day. They realize that they are not doing well compared to their classmates—and their peers know it as well (Morgan et al., 2012). The good news is that effective early interventions to increase reading proficiency can produce other positive effects in fifth graders—they will be less likely to self-report as angry, sad, and unpopular.

Children with reading disorders report illnesses in outpatient settings more often, with complaints such as headaches, stomachaches, and nausea (Galuschka & Schulte-Körne, 2016). Twenty percent of children and adolescents with reading disorders also develop anxiety disorders, as well as increased incidence of depression and conduct disorders. Left untreated, students will face increased failure, absenteeism, and reduced psychological well-being as adults.

A study of conduct issues by Morgan, Farkas, Tufis, and Sperling (2008) discovered that being a weak reader in the spring of first grade is a significant predictor of behavior issues in third grade. Early reading failure has a negative impact on future behavior. As third graders, they were more likely to act out, withdraw from class activities, and demonstrate poor self-control. Furthermore, Morgan et al. report that the odds of the same students who were poor readers in first grade continuing to be poor readers in third grade were extraordinarily high.

It's difficult to imagine a more pivotal, vulnerable point in a child's life than when they are learning to read. The kind of readers that children become will impact much of their lives—and it's happening at the tender ages of 5–7 years. Decisions educators and parents make at this pivotal point can catapult students to success or accelerate the propensity for less positive outcomes. Effective interventions as early as possible to prevent reading failure can play a monumental role in the lives of students.

Adults who are not good readers fare poorly. According to the advocacy group ProLiteracy (Adult Literacy Facts, 2019), 70% of welfare recipients in the United States have low literacy levels. They are much less likely to be employed and, when they are, make much lower wages and are more apt to be hurt on the job. Since they are much less likely to pay taxes and more apt to receive benefits, other taxpayers pay a price of around $225 billion per year in terms of reduced economic productivity. Lack of reading skills contributes heavily to the poverty cycle. A child of parents with low levels of literacy has a depressing 72% chance of having that same low level. And health issues are a bigger concern for weak readers than more literate citizens, often because they cannot read prescription packaging or a doctor's instructions, and they often feel isolated and suffer low self-esteem as adults (Literacy Foundation, 2019).

It's hard to fathom worse prospects for our poor readers, and yet there's more. There is a definitive link between low reading levels and future incarceration. There's an old urban myth that prison officials plan future cell space needs according to third grade reading scores. Not true—your local prison warden does not examine students' test data to forecast new prison construction. The trouble is, they probably could.

A study found that 80% of Texas inmates were functionally illiterate (Moody et al., 2000), with deficiencies in single-word decoding and reading comprehension. Bruner's (1993) research lays out the case that academic failure and delinquency are tightly connected, and that the underpinning is reading failure. Furthermore, this ongoing failure to read and learn develops into long-term frustration that can build into delinquent behaviors. In addition, a high percentage of those in juvenile detention, Bruner reports, were diagnosed at school as having learning disabilities, when in fact they did not have neurological abnormalities. This scathing report from the U.S. Department of Justice implores educators to adjust reading methods in light of the failures of so many students. A particularly brutal part of the report: compulsory attendance may even harm some of these students. Compulsory attendance, designed to ensure literacy in every child, can have quite the opposite effect. Intense, sustained frustration over the inability to read well, without positive resolution, can damage children. This is an older report—1993—but includes familiar pleas about using science-based methods to teach reading.

SOME GOOD NEWS

The responsibility to ensure that students become proficient readers is daunting. What educators do every day in classrooms is amazingly influential. How reading is taught impacts entire lives—including careers, income, and even psychological and physical well-being. The good news is that improving children's reading is quite doable. A summary of research reveals that science-based reading instruction can prevent or correct a majority of reading difficulties and disabilities (Kirkpatrick, 2015). And while not every reading difficulty can be totally eliminated, even students with significant issues can read much better with effective instruction. In one study Kirkpatrick discusses, almost 40% of students with severe reading disabilities no longer needed special education services in reading. Imagine how the trajectories of students' lives will be changed by becoming proficient readers.

In addition to the power of science-based reading instruction, technology is available now to support many of our students with reading disabilities. Spell-checkers, audio textbooks, and word predictors are familiar tools. Now, students can record what is being said with smart pens equipped with cameras for notes that transfer to a computer. Tablets can, at a tap, enable text-to-speech and allow students to dictate entire essays or answer homework questions. These tools provide students with the freedom to show what they have learned in different ways and provide workarounds for disabilities. Other tools are designed for instruction. There are apps for fluency in which teachers can tape stories that allow students to engage in repeated reading, and apps for phonics practice.

SEE THEIR STRENGTHS

In the midst of this justifiable push to improve reading proficiency lies something else of great import—seeing the gifts of struggling readers. In the same way that many ADHD and ELL students have wonderful talents, our imperiled readers bring gifts into classrooms and beyond. The frustrating struggle to read and learn—to just do what the other children are doing quite readily—is obvious. The gifts—what they excel at—can get buried in the reading rubble.

In Malcolm Gladwell's (2013) wonderful book *David and Goliath*, he talks about the extraordinary number of successful entrepreneurs with dyslexia. Discount brokerage founder Charles Schwab and the CEO of Cisco, John Chambers, are just two. Gladwell poses a question about why so many dyslexics are highly successful: are they just so smart that the disability couldn't stop them, or did the constant struggle provide some advantage in life? According to *USA Today* writer Edward C. Baig (2018), dyslexic billionaire Richard Branson was beaten regularly by his headmaster for his poor reading. An article on CNBC.com by Alexandria Gibbs (2017) reported that the headmaster (now famously) remarked that Branson would either wind up as a millionaire—or in jail. (There is actually a research-based rationale for his comments, however inappropriate.) In an article by Baig (2018), Branson does in fact credit much of his success to the disability. Furthermore, Baig contends that the wiring in the dyslexic brain may enable more creative thinking than typically wired brains.

Daymond John, clothing line entrepreneur and one of the "sharks" on the television program "Shark Tank," recalls not being able to spell his middle name and the fatigue of reading—but he excelled in math and science. He credits his parents, his ability to focus on his strengths, and a co-op program at his high school in which he could work one week and attend school the next. Still today, John has difficulty interpreting signs on hotel walls about the location of his room and asks others to review important readings (Glader, 2019). It's not just entrepreneurs—entertainers such as Jay Leno and Tom Cruise, economists, scientists, and even writers emerge as highly successful dyslexics. A common thread emerges in their stories: the support of others and the triumph of the human spirit over adversity. They were helped by family members urging them on, kitchen table talks about perseverance, and finding things they could excel in, such as business, sports, or even writing.

These accounts of real-world triumphs over reading adversity are inspiring. But many of our weak readers encounter much bleaker situations. And many of our students lack the support systems that these highly successful individuals enjoyed. Clearly, developing proficient readers from kindergarten through graduation is too big a topic for one chapter in one book. In a perfect world, students would arrive on the doorstep of kindergarten ready to read. Many don't. In a perfect world, students' brains would all be wired to readily unlock the reading code, to convert symbols to sounds. They are not. But here is what educators have: an abundance of science about what works best in developing proficient readers.

RESEARCH TO PRACTICE

Before we even meet students in kindergarten, they have already been significantly impacted by preschool literacy practices. The advantages of having parents or caretakers who consistently expose their children to literature is so significant that community initiatives to instill these practices are worth every effort. Stakeholders from pediatricians to parents to the local library can impact reading and vocabulary. The good news is that, wherever children are when they arrive, educators are equipped with solid research about thoughtfully developing good readers. And while lower-grade teachers do much of the initial heavy lifting, reading is a K–12 undertaking. Every teacher engages students in text; therefore, every educator is a reading teacher. And while educators understandably worry about reading test scores, developing successful readers impacts lives and communities. Low literacy is a key predictor of poverty, poor health, and even incarceration. Reading changes lives. So, what's in *your* reading plan?

QUESTIONS TO PONDER

- On learning walks through your buildings, how much are students reading?
- In this week's lesson plans, is time carved out for student reading?
- Is every teacher in your building well versed in effective reading practices?
- Are strengths of weaker readers being recognized?

- Are students being assessed very early for reading difficulties? Is that data being utilized to improve reading?
- Is technology being utilized to enable students to compensate for reading difficulties?
- What is being done in your community to spread the word about the power of reading to preschool children?

MOVING FORWARD

➤ Jot down ideas for building reading proficiency in every reader. Also, consider ideas for uncovering and developing strengths of these students. _____

_____

_____

_____

_____

CHAPTER 4

Trapped in an Age-Based System

I n the 2019 Wimbledon tennis tournament, 15-year-old Cori "Coco" Gauff captivated the world's attention. Not yet old enough to drive, she defeated veteran Venus Williams and advanced to win in two subsequent matches in the tournament. Her father, a former college basketball player, serves as her head coach, but Coco is surrounded by other top-tier coaches and professionals to support her developing talents. Many rightfully marvel at the commitment to excellence and incredibly hard work that goes into developing this level of talent. But what if Coco had been relegated to a system in which she could only compete against players her own age? What if she had to routinely pair up with students just learning the backhand? What if this elite athlete had to patiently complete practice work on court dimensions or listen to a review on how to keep score? Furthermore, what if Coco had to endure a stigma for being allowed to read ahead or leave the room to work for a while with others at her talent level? Imagine if officials at Wimbledon had barred her from competing due to her young age, under the guise of fairness or even social development, saying that she should not be on the court with older players. Would people be outraged that this young woman was being held back?

Consider if the same mind-set often applied to developing athletic talents—letting them soar—applied to academic achievement. Evidence suggests that many gifted and talented students are trapped in an age-based, lockstep system in which academic content is delivered at the same pace to gifted students as to general and special education students.

It may seem odd for gifted learners to be included in a conversation about students not reaching their potential or being vulnerable. In fact, the common belief that teachers, leaders, and parents don't need to worry much about this group is a myth. But how could they not be OK at school, when they are endowed with unique intellectual and/or creative gifts? Some never get on the radar for gifted support, which alone places them at risk for not reaching their potential. Others are classified as gifted but are not provided with academic opportunities that stretch their intellectual capacities; rather, they do the same work as everyone else. And some gifted students encounter issues like perfectionism and not fitting in at school that warrant attention.

TRAITS OF GIFTEDNESS

The most common traits of giftedness show how these learners are unique (Webb, Gore, Amend, & DeVries, 2007). These students grasp concepts quickly, remember well, think abstractly, and have a talent for intense concentration. They may even teach themselves to read and write before entering school. Problem-solving questioners with a high level of intellectual curiosity, they typically have large vocabularies and vivid imaginations. They often enjoy experimenting and doing things on their own. But they also can be quite sensitive, idealistic, and deeply affected by events, including injustices around the world.

But some of the same traits that make schoolwork easier for this group can create challenges in the classroom. Their ability to catch on quickly combined with often keen memory and fast recall might result in restless behavior and frequent interruptions, which can be mistakenly perceived as attention issues. Original ideas might be viewed as oppositional. And their self-reliance and the sheer volume of information they are carrying around can cause a perception of audaciously questioning authority figures. Their cognitive strengths are often out of sync with their chronological age and size, creating a potential mismatch with peers. Often self-reliant, they might balk at working with others, and may correct classmates—and even teachers and leaders. Their curious, questioning nature can be off-putting and may seem like arrogance or disrespect. Although their road may appear to be easy, gifted students might be struggling in school more than we realize. Just because they are completing work—which could mean doing the minimum to play the game of school—does not mean that they are getting the education they need to reach their potential.

Betts and Neihart (1988) created specific profiles of gifted and talented (G/T) students. One of these profiles, which includes 90% of students in gifted programs, describes students who have figured out what educators and parents want from them and largely deliver. These students score high on tests, behave appropriately, and gain approval from adults. The authors contend that this large group superficially appears to be doing just fine. The risk, however, is that complacency and boredom sink in and they learn to do the minimum of what is expected. They largely go through the motions of school, are liked by peers, and don't appear vulnerable, but fail to develop intellectual autonomy or pursue individual interests. In a university setting or in the real world, they are well adjusted but may not reach their potential.

Creative, divergent thinkers may take on a different look at school—which can appear as noncompliance. Often missed as candidates for gifted programs, these students tend to question authority, be adept at sarcasm, and exhibit nonconformity. The lack of acknowledgment of their talents may increase their frustration, making them more likely to be at risk for behaviors such as taking drugs and dropping out as they get older. Betts and Neihart (1988) created another profile at particular risk, students whose exceptional gifts are masked by learning disabilities or who have emotional or physical handicaps. Their obvious deficits, such as off-task behavior or messy work, can send them down a path toward a more remedial education, rather than a development of their strengths. A focus on deficits can obscure students' exceptional qualities and alter academic trajectories.

Understanding that giftedness can look different than what might be expected and including more students, such as creative thinkers and those with disabilities, is important to making interventions more accessible. Gifted individuals often need a different type of instruction in order to thrive, particularly those at risk of dropping out. A bored, restless student who might be described as a "handful" might warrant further examination for giftedness.

SCOPE

About 6% of the nation's schoolchildren, according to the Office for Civil Rights (2012), are considered gifted and talented. What may be surprising is that the federal government does not provide funds for G/T programs. (The one exception is federal funding to serve traditionally underrepresented groups.) This means that services for these students are almost entirely paid for by state and local governments. Some states, however, don't allocate any funds for gifted and talented programs, leaving this decision up to individual districts and creating a patchwork of G/T programs across the country. The Davidson Institute (n.d.) provides an online chart that demonstrates the range of gifted programs by state. In some states, programs are mandated and fully funded and in others the funding is either partial or nonexistent.

In addition to funding variations, methods of identifying and serving G/T students vary by state. A chart of state mandates for gifted students is located at Hoagies' Gifted Education Page (n.d.). Examples of offerings include individual education plans, dual enrollment, and early kindergarten entry. In sum, the commitment to serving G/T students and the models utilized vary significantly. Even what it means to be gifted varies by state.

Why does this variance matter? For one thing, the lack of uniformity makes tracking progress challenging. Conversations about potential are equally challenging, because what is the potential for a G/T student? One can easily argue that high school graduation rates alone set the bar too low for any of our students, but at least that measure is readily available. These students will likely pass state tests—but is that success? Another gauge is entering a four-year university, but that is often the minimum expectation for these students.

Some experts contend that the nation's laser-like attention on struggling learners has diverted attention away from developing the talents of gifted learners (Neihart, Pfeiffer, & Cross, 2016). We currently have fewer gifted programs, a decreased number of children served, and even less professional development for teachers, as well as more gifted students being served solely in general education classrooms. Every educator is aware of federal laws that protect students with disabilities.

Individual education plans are constructed and reviewed, and testing accommodations are carefully planned and implemented by testing coordinators. Do the unique qualities of gifted students need similar protections? Many advocates believe they do, because federal law would provide services across the country, so that some students—simply due to geography—are not allowed to languish in a learning environment where they already know much of the content, idly waiting for other students to catch up to them.

SERVING GIFTED AND TALENTED STUDENTS

VanTassel-Baska (2005) provides a pragmatic list of nonnegotiables for districts to consider in supporting G/T students in reaching their potential. A common theme is to let their abilities and progress, rather than age, guide decisions. Accelerated learning, further detailed below, is a cornerstone of this approach. Early entrance to (and exit from) school includes skipping a grade for students who are two years ahead of peers. This advancement can remedy the holding pattern often seen in middle school. Dual enrollment, advanced placement (AP) and International Baccalaureate (IB) programs, and online courses provide additional supports. In the heterogeneous classroom, gifted students should have more advanced work; for example, some might be analyzing different texts or solving more advanced math programs. Unfortunately, much research suggests that most classrooms remain largely undifferentiated for gifted students, as teachers focus on covering the same material with the whole class (Colangelo, Assouline, & Gross, 2004; VanTassel & Basks, 2005).

THE CASE FOR MOVING ON

Perhaps ironically, the old one-room schoolhouse model may have functioned better for gifted students than today's settings. In that learning environment, teachers taught multiple ages and levels in a common space, and students were encouraged to move to the next level of learning as they were able. Today's schools use more rigid groups based on age rather than ability. The case for moving students on to an appropriate level is made in a compelling report by Colangelo, Assouline, and Cross (2004) that lays out how American schools are holding back the brightest students by not moving them on to a higher grade, subject level, or early college entry.

They argue that accelerating highly capable students is one of the most effective interventions available—and it costs nothing. (Martin Luther King Jr., they mention, graduated high school at the age of 15.) They also advocate for early kindergarten for some students, and, for profoundly gifted students, skipping more than one grade. They contend that an age-based curriculum is a mismatch for learners who could advance faster. Boredom and unhappiness at school can result. In addition, gifted students are often a better social match with older students. Equity, after all, is not a synonym for sameness.

An exhaustive publication titled *A Nation Empowered* outlines the research and practice for accelerating gifted students. This online reference guides supports schools in implementing acceleration methods that are evidence based and cost effective, as well as identifying barriers such as bureaucratic pitfalls. As part of this work, Southern and Jones (2015) list 20 ways to accelerate gifted students. One approach is to match students with content that is more intellectually appropriate. For example, some students may physically move to a higher-level classroom for science, math, or language arts and then return to their home class for other activities. Similarly, the content may come to them; in other words, a student could have a different math curriculum but remain in the same classroom with peers. A different approach is to compact the curriculum within the classroom, so that gifted students partake in less drill and practice, and move at a faster pace. For some students, entering school early or skipping grades entirely might be appropriate acceleration. For older students, dual enrollment, AP courses, and summer programs for gifted students serve to accelerate their learning.

In sum, acceleration can counter the industrial educational framework of age-based, lockstep education. These high-ability students spend much of their days practicing work they already know how to do and sitting through reviews of information they have already mastered (Cross, Andersen, & Mammadov, 2015).

PULL-OUT PROGRAMS

Some districts pull G/T students out of their regular classrooms for enrichment. The question is: what are gifted students doing in the pull-out time? Are they advancing in content or developing thinking skills? Barshaw (2019) reports that a survey of 2,000 elementary students showed that gifted students were not being exposed to much advanced content; rather, they were learning the same things as their nongifted classmates. Instead of moving forward into new areas of study, time was largely spent on critical thinking and creativity, such as debates and projects. In fact, out of 26 items of study, advanced math ranked 18th and advanced reading was 19th. Leadership and social-emotional learning activities ranked much higher. The survey reveals that teachers were individually making decisions about what gifted students would be learning—there was no set district curriculum for the classes. Additionally, while students were selected for the G/T program largely based on math and reading scores, sparse advanced instruction was being provided in those areas. In examining test scores for over 350,000 students, Barshaw also found that while gifted students' growth is slower than it should be, higher gains tend to come from a combination of acceleration and enrichment.

In a small study in New York, state test results for two groups of gifted students were analyzed (Ruggiero, 2012). One group engaged in a gifted two-hour-a-week pull-out program. Because the other school did not have a gifted program, teachers provided the names of students they believed would have qualified for one. After instruction, the scores were statistically the same on the statewide test. The author cautions that the test might not have included content studied in the pull-out, and that the program was part-time. Of course, the teacher in the general education classroom in the school without the gifted program may have implemented high-level lessons. Even so, the pull-out group did not receive higher scores than the group that remained in class.

THE GIFTED DROPOUT

The fact that some gifted students fail to complete high school is perplexing, since they are typically equipped for learning. The numbers are difficult to nail down, because definitions of "gifted" vary across the country and, as mentioned before, some states do not have separate G/T programs. Robertson (1991) estimates that somewhere between 18% and 25% of gifted students fail to finish high school. Others contend that the number is much lower, or that it cannot be accurately gauged. With less than 10% of learners even classified as gifted, this group may not be on the radar as vulnerable to dropout.

According to Renzulli and Park (2002), certain factors increase the likelihood of G/T students dropping out of school. Students from lower SES families, for example, constitute almost half of gifted dropouts. In addition, a significant relationship exists between parents' educational level and the child dropping out. For gifted children who drop out, a high percentage of their parents either did not complete high school or only completed high school. Cross (2018) contends that the largest achievement gap among all students is in the low-SES gifted group. There was some indication that parents' academic expectations were not as high as those of other parents of gifted students. In addition, ethnic minority gifted students drop out at a higher rate (Renzulli & Park, 2002). Some gifted students, however, decided to leave school over the frustration resulting from lack of recognition, which can fuel bitterness and anger as well as feelings of rejection and decreased self-esteem. They no longer fit in at school or see no relevance in continuing (Betts & Neihart, 1988).

Perhaps surprisingly, gifted students commonly dropped out due to course failure (a reminder that these learners are not gifted in every subject). A dislike of school was also indicated. The authors' recommendations on averting gifted dropout? The first is to develop a watch list of gifted students at risk of dropping out. Next, address the special academic needs of the group and strengthen teacher-student relationships. Participation in extracurricular activities has proven helpful, as well as fostering parental involvement (Renzulli & Park, 2002).

SOCIAL-EMOTIONAL ELEMENTS

One characteristic of gifted learners is that their development is often asynchronous, or at different stages. Their unique cognitive development is often far beyond their physical or emotional range for their age. Intellectual conversations with adults, for example, might feel more suitable for them than with classmates. Their motor skills and size may be in line with their age mates, but their intellectual range may extend far beyond their classmates. This mismatch of development combined with a sense that peers view them differently create a need for educators to facilitate nurturing relationships in safe classrooms (Neihart et al., 2014). Out-of-sync development, Blass (2014) argues, can cause social isolation within their age group, with whom they often have little in common, and even increase underachievement, since these students may conceal their abilities as a trade-off to secure friends.

Being stigmatized for being gifted is a concern among some gifted students. Coping mechanisms for gifted learners vary (Cross, 2018). Some try to blend in and avoid standing out at school. Another student might play the role of the stereotypical "nerd" as a deflection. Yet other students purposefully underachieve to fit in. Some pretend to be less talented to avoid hurting peers' feelings. African American gifted students are particularly vulnerable. Academic success can signal, particularly in secondary grades, an almost cultural betrayal on their part. These learners may encounter negative peer pressure from the larger African American student body to resist intellectual giftedness on the misperceived grounds that academic success is a component of white culture (Neihart et al., 2016).

Social dynamics may prove more challenging for gifted students as they enter the middle school years. They may feel less accepted than they did in elementary grades, as athleticism becomes increasingly desirable among the student body. Students lacking interest in sports might have fewer opportunities to form friendships at school. In addition, some studies have indicated that gifted students are more likely to be introverted in general. Teachers should exercise caution in publicly praising these students' exceptional gifts in front of the class—which can understandably lead to gifted students having fewer classroom relationships. Private recognition might prove more beneficial (Neihart et al., 2014).

In addition to these challenges, some evidence exists that gifted students may have heightened perfectionism and a related fear of failure. It is difficult to know if this trait is really more prevalent among gifted students, due to the various definitions of giftedness and ways of measuring perfectionism. But the trait has been associated with giftedness for many years. A study by Schuler (2000) discusses two types of perfectionists: normal and neurotic. Students in the normal perfectionist group focused on doing their best and felt supported by teachers, friends, and parents. They also used order and organization to manage stress levels. They were typically described by teachers as conscientious, hard-working, and organized. They viewed themselves as high-ability students and felt the key to success was hard work and a drive for perfection. When they failed to reach their expectations or experienced failure, they worked harder. Normal perfectionism has some positive aspects for student growth.

By contrast, the neurotic perfectionists anxiously fixated on their mistakes. Rather than viewing perfection as doing one's best, they worried incessantly about messing up or making mistakes. Errors, to this group, caused worries that perhaps they were not that smart after all. Mistakes brought embarrassment—they experienced intense concern over mistakes and even replayed the events in their minds. Highly self-critical, they expected perfection and became angry with themselves when they fell short. Interestingly, both groups of perfectionists expressed an intense dislike for receiving grades as a group with peers who did not care about their work, and they resented having to explain material that was easy for them. They did, however, enjoy working in groups of similar ability, but lamented the lack of those opportunities. The message for educators from this study: there is a continuum of perfectionism. One end has some positive traits of perfectionism. But the neurotic perfectionist, they caution, is in an almost constant state of anxiety and need for approval. Teachers modeling coping strategies and effective handling of failure, stress management techniques, and counseling are just some steps to support these learners. In addition, educators can support perfectionist students in setting more realistic goals. A minority of gifted students fall in this range of perfectionism, but their ability to pretend to be perfect may make it harder for educators to see their distress (Schuler, 2000).

GROUPING CONSIDERATIONS IN HETEROGENEOUS CLASSROOMS

Gifted students are most often situated in heterogeneous classrooms. Fortunately, the days of quiet cemetery rows in which students sit in isolation have largely passed. My many classroom observations confirm that learning today includes collaborative work as an integral part of most lessons. But all groups are not equal. Effective grouping requires clear purpose and structure—simply pulling desks together does not ensure learning. For example, students might get grouped to practice four math problems. But as soon as the fastest-processing student gets an answer, everyone stops—why continue? This robs the other students of adequate processing time to get the answer on their own and creates a situation in which the gifted kids skate by.

In some situations, heterogeneous grouping works well. For example, if student projects today require a graphic designer, an editor, a videographer, and a sports statistician, you might allow students the opportunity to choose their job based on their perceived expertise. In math, informal, flexible groupings may pair one student who's almost there with one who's more solid on the concept, but those pairings are likely to change in the next day or so as skills develop.

There are also times when it's entirely appropriate to group high-ability students together. For example, if observations reveal that four students have reached conceptual understanding and require no further practice, move them on to a group with more challenging tasks, or a new concept entirely. In language arts, provide different novels for advanced readers with a range of choices. In social studies, encourage (monitored) independent study when students are ready. In science, high-ability students can easily work together on an extension of the standard, creating real-world solutions to problems. (Simply providing gifted learners with more work is never the appropriate path.)

Teachers may feel reluctant to group advanced learners together. Gifted students often get distributed around the class as sort of anchors for group work. It is important to remember that differentiated instruction applies to high-ability instruction, too. Often our attention (understandably) is on struggling learners, who are always on the radar of good teachers. They require additional attention in class, and in meetings teachers hear about the urgency of moving struggling learners to proficiency on high-stakes tests. But it's not the job of high-ability students to teach emerging learners or to keep another learner on task.

In addition, gifted learners may tend to simply knock out the work themselves, which may relegate other learners to the sidelines. How much did the other learners engage in the work? Gifted students benefit from opportunities to stretch their own intellectual wings with other exceptional thinkers who work at their rapid pace. If their work on the current learning target demonstrates proficiency before the rest of the class, the instructional responsibility is to move them on.

It's understandable why gifted students often dislike group work. The pace may be slow, the tasks may be too easy, and they might worry about protecting their grades by taking charge of the group. The purpose of groups, in my view, is to process new information, practice, research, and share ideas in order to be better prepared for individual work. Any grades should be given for the independent work each student does subsequent to the group. For example, if groups are examining different writings of Edgar Allan Poe, after the collaborative work, each student should prepare an individual product that demonstrates understanding of the learning target. Jigsaws, in which each student first works independently and then teaches their portion of a topic, can be an effective way to mingle gifted students into groups. They are structured so that students research and discover information on their own first, which provides a layer of autonomous work for gifted students. Jigsaws can be managed so that gifted students have the same focus of study and first get time with like-ability students before heading to the heterogenous groups for future discussions.

MORE OF THE SAME

How much review and multiple exposures students need for a concept varies by learner. For example math teachers may assume that all students need a review of last year's concepts to lay the groundwork for the new concept about to be taught. Gifted students often have exceptional memories and may not require this review, and thus find the repetition and slow pace frustrating. Similarly, as standardized testing closes in, another round of review ensues. Ongoing formative assessments, such as quick checks, portfolios, and end of lesson summaries, can remedy these situations. In a review "boot camp" I observed, students who required no review were grouped together for rich extensions.

Boring, monotonous work can trigger stress, frustration, and even anger in gifted students (Kaplan, 1990). Students will not be happy going through the motions of simple activities. When they finish their work faster than other learners, they should not be given more of the same. Menus with choices are a more productive path for all learners. Students can select from a range of products that capture their intellectual imaginations, which should have levels of difficulty and thinking. While advanced material for gifted students is most commonly delivered through differentiation within the general education classroom, there is a common belief that gifted students do not require differentiation (Plucker & Callahan, 2014). In particular, advanced readers are not provided with opportunities at their level in regular classrooms. Struggling students are given more differentiated instruction than gifted ones.

When in doubt, ask gifted learners—for that matter, all learners—what they need to learn better. The ability of gifted students to crank out work can mask dissatisfaction with class, and lead to not just weak work habits but a loss of potential. Their questioning nature, in addition, should not be construed as an affront to the authority of teachers or leaders. Langrehr (2019) describes creative thinking as the ability to see new solutions apart from the dominant patterns stored in our brains. The world—and certainly a school—needs creative solutions. The combination of unique ideas gifted students express and talents beyond our own might make it seem like the balance is off—after all, we are the experts, right? But they are just children, even the older ones. They need to be nurtured and developed in safe classrooms in which their special gifts can thrive and grow.

RESEARCH MEETS PRACTICE

Rather than a cohesive national focus for gifted and talented students, a patchwork quilt of definitions, qualifications, and educational services exists. Some states have no mandates for supporting gifted students at all. This lack of national structure makes it difficult to gather data on how the brightest among us are progressing. In addition, a myth persists that gifted and talented students require no special considerations—that they will be fine on their own. We know that this is not true.

To develop the talents of G/T students, schools need to employ both acceleration and enrichment of content. Differentiated instruction in the general education classroom should be the mainstay, not the exception for gifted students. Evidence suggests that a heavy focus on struggling learners drives instruction. But every learner's needs are important—the needs of gifted students cannot be set aside in our quest to move struggling learners' achievement scores. In addition, experts in the gifted field contend that relying on gifted students to bolster scores might influence the lack of acceleration to more intellectually matched content. In other words, there may be a belief that if these students are studying advanced concepts, they will miss practice on grade-level concepts that will be on high-stakes tests. Pull-out programs that focus on creative thinking may be helpful, but limited time might reduce opportunities for advanced content exploration. Acceleration, experts contend, has a plethora of evidence-based support and is cost effective.

It might be helpful to reflect on our beliefs and practices related to gifted students. It would be difficult to find even one educator who disagrees that struggling students or students with disabilities should have support. Similarly, ESL support is routinely accepted. Are we also open to the idea of allowing a different math educator to teach a small group an advanced concept within the heterogeneous classroom? Should it be routine for a small group to leave the classroom for a science experiment down the hall as it is for students to leave for extra help? Would a high school teacher be welcomed in classrooms to work with sixth grade students?

Years ago, I was visiting an elementary classroom that had a wide range of reading levels. Recognizing this, the teacher provided different resources for higher readers. During reading time, the higher readers slipped quietly into the hallway and read silently. This group became informally known as "hall readers." This allowed, the teacher believed, additional focus with readers who could benefit from more teacher assistance. After a while, the practice abruptly stopped. Parents of students who did not get to be hall readers complained to the principal that this was not a fair practice. All the students should get to work in the hall. But, to revisit the opening example of the young tennis star, where would she be today if she had not been allowed to soar—to be a hall reader?

QUESTIONS TO PONDER

- Does your district or school allow early kindergarten entry for gifted students?
- Does your school currently accelerate students to content that is more intellectually appropriate, such as allowing a third grader to take fifth-grade math?
- Does your school allow G/T students to skip grades entirely?
- If your school has a pullout program for gifted students, does it include creative thinking pursuits or advanced content?
- Is instruction in general education classrooms differentiated for G/T students?

- Does your district have active AP and dual enrollment programs?
- At your school, is there an appropriate balance between supporting gifted students and struggling learners?

MOVING FORWARD

➤ What is the mission of gifted programs in your district? Is this mission being realized? Are there more students who should be considered for gifted programs? What are your personal perceptions of gifted students and their potential? _____

_____

_____

_____

_____

Resource suggestion: Todd Stanley is an expert on education for gifted students. He posts many free resources he has created on his website, MyEdExpert (https://www.MyEdExpert.com).

CHAPTER 5

Hanging by a Thread

From kindergarten to graduation is a long journey. Students learn to read, to count, and to write. There are chapter books, timed multiplication tests, and paragraph construction. The middle school transition proves rocky for many—the content moves faster and deeper, with more teachers, departments, and challenges. Ninth grade: the toughest transition of all comes. Even students who did well in middle school often flounder. There are countless ways students might falter: fall behind, fail classes, lose interest, and even give up. Lists of students in danger who need intervention are kept. Many times, the same names appear year after year. But new names emerge. Some keep plugging away; other students keep coming to school simply because they must.

Students who are behind academically are in peril of not graduating, which places them in a group particularly vulnerable to not reaching their potential. What we do with this group of students matters greatly. As they mature, the gaps often grow. Course failures mount, and missing credits mean they won't graduate with their friends, a shameful realization. Some become disconnected from learning and from peers—it gets harder to face school. Others hang in there on academics but face other pressing issues. Despite all the information students hear about the negatives of leaving school, they hit the exits. It's not a high school problem—it's a K–12 problem, because some of the factors contributing to dropout start much earlier. The conundrum schools face is how to maintain high academic standards without losing kids or impacting them in unintended ways. The good news is that schools are trying innovative approaches to an old problem—to keep students engaged in learning so that they graduate and have a shot at reaching their potential. But old ideas that have proven ineffective continue to cycle through our systems, such as grade-level retention.

THE IRONY OF RETENTION

In a collective fervor to hold children accountable for their learning, 16 states require that third graders who do not meet reading expectations be retained or held back in third grade. The logic behind these retentions is that students who are not reading by third grade are more likely to eventually drop out of high school. In some states, students can avoid retention with an intervention program. In other states, retention is allowed, but not mandated (Education Commission of the States, 2016). The irony in these policies is that grade-level retention is often linked to higher dropout rates and other detrimental effects. The well-intentioned zeal to create readers may have unintended negative effects on children.

Across grade levels, even with younger students, the practice does not produce academic rewards (Anderson, Whipple, & Jimerson, 2003). Young children might show a short-lived improvement, but the retained students' scores tend to decline below those of their equally low-performing peers who were socially promoted. Long-term, these retained children are much more likely to drop out of high school—2 to 11 times more likely than promoted students. Retention may fail to motivate students to work harder. In a survey of sixth graders on twenty stressors in life, they placed their fear of being retained just behind the loss of a parent or going blind. Furthermore, retained students are more likely to act out in class, display aggressive behavior, and be suspended or expelled. Boys, minority students, and students with learning disabilities are the ones more likely to be retained. This is not a handful of students—an estimated 2.4 million in the United States every single year are retained in grade level. Retention is also an expensive proposition; since students are repeating the same grade, taxpayers pay for the additional year.

Back in 2003, Florida was the first state to implement a reading plan that included retention as a component. Other states followed suit. Using the FCAT (their state test) as the bar, Florida held back over 23,000 students the first year. In the beginning, improvements occurred. But a longitudinal study revealed both the high costs and the disappointing academic results of this plan (Jasper, 2016). First, the costs: in the first year, taxpayers paid $84 million to retain those 23,000 students. From 2003 to 2013, Florida retained a total of about 160,000 third graders, costing an estimated $587 million in full-time equivalent funds. Although the study showed short-term gains soon after remediation, these gains disappeared, and reading scores dropped, with 65% scoring at level one on the FCAT. In 2010–2011, 93% of the retained students were still below proficiency. Of the original 23,000-plus retained that first year, 41% did not graduate with a standard diploma. The unfortunate finding of this study of Florida's A+ Plan: the students who were held back in the name of reading largely stayed behind in reading, and at significant financial cost. This study, like other reports, reveals that retention disproportionately impacts boys, minority children, and low-SES students. Education departments gather a burgeoning amount of ongoing data on student performance, from benchmark tests to standardized tests. The purpose of that data, we are frequently advised, is to make positive instructional decisions to help students. Does retaining students due to lagging reading skills result in improved educational futures? According to this research, no. Retention, the case can be argued, is not much of an instructional plan. It's not a new idea. In fact, studies go back over a century on the impacts of grade-level retention. Over a long period of time, retention has largely been shown not to be effective for academics or students' social-emotional needs (Anderson et al., 2013).

An interesting sidebar is this research: retention is practiced more in public than private schools (Jasper, 2016). And while no reasons are given, one must imagine that private school parents might be reluctant to write another tuition check in order for their child to repeat the same work. In that financial scenario, other solutions are explored. In public schools, taxpayers are also writing a check—they just may not know it.

Retention, to some, feels instinctively appropriate, perhaps to send an emphatic message to students and parents to get with it—we mean business on these reading scores! Some hold that it will motivate kids—that if we tell children that this awful thing might befall them, they'll read harder and faster. Or they truly believe that it's beneficial for a child to spend another year in the same place. And while students certainly need to bear responsibility for their learning, retention based on reading scores tends to place the bulk of the blame (and shame) for deficiencies on the students' shoulders. In one state using retention as a reading intervention, the governor himself was retained in school and felt it did him some good, and thus he advocated for the practice. Newer research about retention looks a lot like the old research from many years ago (Jimerson, 2001). There is no lack of research to analyze—more research is not needed. Jimerson's view, therefore, is that conversations about fixing academic issues need to move on to other ideas. And while social promotion is not a popular option, his vast pool of research indicates that it's preferable to retention.

At the least, retention as a method of improving reading is worthy of big conversations. Reading includes a complex set of skills within the brain. Plus, learning to read has many variables, such as whether children are read to at home, SES, vocabulary, and the presence of dyslexia. And while the educational system often may seem like an assembly-line approach, children's brains don't work like an assembly line.

Other instructional options must be explored. That might include ensuring that instructional resources and practices are science based. Additional instructional time might be carved out before school, during Saturday sessions, or in summer programs. Small-group or tutoring sessions, computer apps that add novelty, or incorporating more hands-on activities might be deployed. Previewing vocabulary words, increased guided oral reading, high-interest text, choices of what text to read—what's the plan for reading for each child?

In my experience, it's more challenging to find actual numbers for students retained in middle school, but the impacts on students are readily available. Secondary students who have been retained have increased levels of alcohol use, low self-esteem, drug abuse, self-harm, violence, and in general are less emotionally healthy (Jimerson & Renshaw, 2012). In high school, students can just repeat one course to catch up. In middle and elementary grades, they lose an entire year. It is a myth that retention in lower grades does less harm—across the board, retention is not a viable solution to students who are behind academically.

In middle grades, the criteria for retention have a bigger range. In a district in which I worked, for example, students had to at least pass math, English language arts, and one more core subject, plus have a combined passing average. The difficulty was that to avoid retention, students had to attend a summer credit recovery course with a price tag of a few hundred dollars. Registration was filled with lines of tearful parents with little hope of gathering those funds. Stories of lost jobs and broken-down cars mixed with pleas not to retain their children. Yes, they were aware that their child did not complete the project, do the homework, make up a test, and so forth. There was absolutely no doubt that our poorest families were the hardest hit—their children got retained. The ones who could muster the cash and had transportation recovered the credit.

The failure math didn't add up for taxpayers either; retaining students resulted in significantly higher costs to taxpayers the next year. From a district standpoint, a free summer program might have saved the district money the next year, rather than paying for all of those retained students. Whatever lesson parents and students were taught was also paid for by taxpayers. This is a philosophical discussion for school districts and tax-payers: Should students who didn't complete a chunk of their schoolwork or failed to show proficiency in a subject be provided with a free summer do-over? The truth is—and I worked on the front lines of academic failure for many years—after students begin to fail, options become decidedly less promising. All intervention efforts, such as tutoring, the first time through a grade or subject are more helpful to students—after failure takes hold, scrambling for less attractive options begins, such as summer programs, retention, and social promotion. Failing classes is but one reason students drop out down the road, albeit a big one.

Removing retention as an option, I believe, enables educators to create more effective solutions for failing students. With effective ongoing assessments, educators largely know which standards students did not master. Modules addressing only those standards can be crafted for a second shot at proficiency. Saturday school or mini classes to shore up standards might avert failure. Some schools use "Maymesters" in which students repeat only what they missed. These approaches mend the broken parts along the way, rather than having students repeat an entire course of year of study.

WHY STUDENTS LEAVE SCHOOL: PUSH, PULL, AND FALL

Doll, Eslami, and Walters (2013) examined large longitudinal studies that track why students leave school, using categories of the ways that students leave school established by prior researchers: factors that push students out, factors that pull students out, and times when they fall out of school. Push and pull factors were originally established by Jordan, Lara, and McPartland (1994). Push factors are situations or policies within the school that caused the decision to leave, such as discipline issues, low state test scores, or low attendance. Pull factors are within the student's domain, such as a pregnancy, or quitting school to get a job due to financial woes. Falling out of school is an added category that encompasses academic struggles leading to disengagement and disillusionment with school (Watt & Roessingh, 1994). With push factors, the school is the agent—the force—behind leaving school. The student is the agent in pull factors. When students fall out of school, there is no clear agent. Rather, these are often circumstances that neither the school nor the student make headway on.

The reasons students leave school early have changed over time. In 1955, for example, over one-third left to get married and 14.5% wanted to join the military. Some 60% gave reasons that fit in the pulled-out category, largely marriage and work. Not that many (26.4%) said that they left because they didn't like school (Doll et al., 2013). By 1979, the reasons for dropping looked different—many fewer left to get married, and close to one-third left because they disliked school. In 1988, over one-half reported not liking school; almost 40% said they were failing, and about a third were behind in schoolwork and could not get along with their teachers. One-fifth of the respondents felt like they didn't belong at school.

Studies during this period revealed new information: for example, Hispanic students experienced more pull factors and also felt less safe at school. African American students felt more push factors, while white students reported greater feelings of not belonging at school or disliking school. What's particularly interesting is that when administrators and teachers were queried about their perceptions of why students were dropping out, there was a big mismatch. Educators thought students were leaving due to family problems and lack of family support when students were actually leaving due to loss of interest in learning and academic difficulties. (Educators pointed to home; home pointed to school.) In 2006, push factors dominated in student responses. Over 40% said they had missed too many days; 38% said they were getting poor grades; and almost one-third couldn't keep up with their schoolwork. A quarter of the respondents could not get along with their teachers, and 20% felt like they didn't belong at school. The top pull factor (40.5%) was that they thought it would be easier to just get a GED (Doll et al., 2013).

The trend since 1955? Clearly, more push factors are being reported. Doll et al. (2013) theorize that higher bars for graduation, the standards movement, and No Child Left Behind legislation in 2001 had an impact. (The highest push rates occurred after NCLB came into effect.) These trends in dropping out tell a story of educational and cultural changes. At one time, students dropped out for marriage or work. Now, a big reason many are checking out of school is pretty straightforward—they are having trouble with their coursework (Doll et al., 2013). And many of our students don't even like coming to school.

In *The Silent Epidemic* (Bridgeland, DiIulio, & Morison, 2006), about a third of students reported having to repeat a grade at some point, and about the same number felt they had little hope of ever meeting graduation requirements. A third reported the pull factor of needing to earn money. But the largest reason—almost half the respondents—for leaving school was disinterest in what was being taught. It was boring and they felt demotivated. The interesting part here is that the students with high GPAs who dropped out gave this as their key reason. Through their eyes, the curriculum lacked real-world purpose and interest. And while students in this category were not expressly gifted, it ties in with what we know about gifted students leaving school. As reported in many studies, absenteeism is a key predictor, including a trend of disengagement at school, not waking up in time for school, long periods of absence, and basically being dragged back to school.

How big is the problem? In the U.S. alone, according to the U.S. Department of Education (2016), over half a million drop out of high school each year. But our graduation rate of 82% today is the best it's been, so why the ongoing urgency? Because in today's world, jobs for those without a minimum of a high school diploma have largely vanished. The military today rarely accepts GEDs. The economic reality is that 18% of our students will have much tougher lives without at least a high school diploma. That's a big number.

STUDENTS AT PARTICULAR RISK

Many schools implement early warning systems to accurately predict which students are at risk of dropping out to help keep them on track. The data historically includes grades, attendance, and sometimes behavior. For example, in a study of four districts in Oregon, Burke (2015) reports that grades eight and nine were pivotal points in future dropout, specifically students with GPAs below 2.0 and attendance rates below 80%. An analysis of three Ohio districts identified reading scores in eighth grade, being suspended more than once, GPA, and credits earned in grades 8 and 9 as predictors (Stuit et al., 2016). A study on Chicago schools (Allensworth, Gwynne, de la Torre, & Moore, 2014) strongly suggests that grades and attendance in middle school best predict high school and college success, even more than test scores, race, or poverty. This report also cautions that some middle school students with high grades falter in high school, dropping to Cs and a decline in attendance. It makes the case that all students need to be closely monitored in ninth grade. In addition, this report stresses the impact of attendance in middle grades as a predictor for high school success. In fact, outcomes were better for attendance gains than test score improvements. In schools with low graduation rates, early warning systems often include other factors, such as overage students, engagement with the criminal justice system, early parenthood, and homelessness (U.S. Department of Education, 2016). For all schools, the items most frequently included were grades, attendance, discipline, and credits earned. Administrators or school counselors were most often the ones tracking student progress, and most checked it weekly. High-poverty schools often employed additional interventions, such as access to social services and mentors. So, while there are general warning signals, it is important to identify factors specific to your school or district.

SUPPORTS TO AVOID FRESHMAN BULGE

So many students fail courses in the ninth grade that it's gotten the nickname "Freshman Bulge" due to the number of students having to repeat courses. The transition from middle school to high school is challenging for many students. The buildings themselves are large and intimidating, along with a bigger student body from other feeder schools, a less personal atmosphere, and more demanding coursework. In addition, students are changing as well. Teenagers during this time are often more reliant on peer approval than on parents. Moving to high school can be an isolating, scary experience.

This tough transition has resulted in innovation by schools, including these efforts (Hanover Research, 2017):

- A Portland Public Schools one-week summer program in which identified students participate with mentors to explore career aspirations, behaviors that bring school success, and outreach to parents. Early indicators are showing a significant increase in the number of these students moving on to grade 10.
- A New Jersey high school has moved to teaching teams, similar to a middle school model. Core teachers plus foreign language are organized within a supportive structure, meeting every four days to examine student data and plan intervention strategies. Students have benefited from the increased structure, plus academics are trending up.
- Summer bridge programs to provide some students with a jump-start for fall in math and ELA.
- Ongoing conversations about high school expectations in middle school, along with visits to the high school and information nights at the high school for parents of middle school students.

Mahoney and Cairnes (1997) explored the relationship between participation in extracurricular activities in middle and high school and dropout rates. In studying seventh to twelfth graders, they found that significantly fewer students dropped out who participated in extracurricular activities, especially athletics. These activities, they contend, have the power to forge more positive connections to school. In contrast to academics, which might emphasize the deficits of some students, extracurricular activities often promote their strengths and interests. In addition, extracurricular events may help students transition to high school. The authors recommend reconsidering any exclusionary policies that may prevent participation in these activities.

Creating a list of students likely to drop out—gathering all that data—is just a starting point. What will be done (possibly differently than in the past) to support these learners? And with the impact of higher academic standards and accountability on dropout, how can schools maintain academic standards without inadvertently pushing students into the dropout line? Beyond academics, what can be done to build connections at school, to help students feel a part of things? When students are on an academic downward slide, efforts to pull them back in with best practices rather than push them out are not easy, but imperative.

RISKY BUSINESS

Learning is indeed risky business. All day long, teachers are asking students to jump in and try something new—something that might bring failure. All students have to muster a little courage and faith to risk failure. Now consider a student who has experienced a lot of failure. It's almost like having a job that you're terrible at, but it's required that you show up every day. It's a marvel that some push through and keep trying. Others put their heads on their desks, find excuses to leave, or barely show up. Deep down, they would love to be successful, but school has become a hurtful place. Why don't they just work harder? Why don't they just buck up and get going? Don't they realize their entire lives are at stake?

Sousa and Tomlinson (2011) tell us that the brain simply does not handle failure well. Its job is to ensure the survival of its owner. That means staying away from the hot stove, in this case learning, because failure is what often happens. Students might fear the sting of making mistakes, so they answer with more trepidation—or not at all. If they feel stress and anxiety during class, their brains send chemicals for relief; unfortunately, those tempering agents also reduce critical thinking skills. Of course, the opposite happens when students experience success in class—endorphins release, boosting moods and processing skills. Young students without a track record of failure tend to jump in, unafraid to take chances. But older students need more assurance that success is likely to follow their attempts and feel a bigger negative impact if they try hard—put in the effort—and then fail (Lumsden, 1994). Failure can result in waning self-efficacy (their confidence in being successful at academic tasks), an increased fear of mistakes and embarrassment, and the construction of self-protective walls. The only remedy is to have some success. But it can't be fake, because disingenuous praise, dumbed-down work, and hovering teachers tapping on their desks reminding them to keep working can add to the shame of failure. These students require fearless teachers with diverse instructional tool kits and rapport to match, because in the wrong instructional hands, they might be relegated to sitting in desks doing tedious, remedial work—and things may worsen.

MATCHING TEACHERS TO STUDENTS

The selection of teachers to assign to students who are at greater risk of failure is of paramount importance. Unfortunately, lower-achieving students, across grade levels, are often exposed to more tedious, low-level tasks. These academically vulnerable students are more apt to be presented with seat work and highly structured tasks that provide few opportunities to engage in creative, interactive thinking (Shearer, Ruddell, & Vogt, 2001). Tedious tasks for students who are hanging by an academic thread is a recipe for failure. Sitting in desks filling out work sheets—or tapping on computer screens—can increase frustration. It also allows students to just disappear in class. These reluctant learners need the opposite of that. Lessons should be thought-provoking, based in the real world, collaborative, and as hands-on as possible. To move them higher requires hand-picked educators with rich instructional tool kits and with the mind-set that these students can still achieve.

In talks to leaders, I present this formula: "Struggling students + struggling teachers = ?" Everyone in the room shouts things like, "Disaster! Terrible fit! Trouble!" Behind closed doors, however, their responses are often quite different. Through a significant number of learning walks, I've seen the research play out. The more remedial, core courses are packed with students doing more teacher-centered, passive, low-level work. Right next door, different students will be engaging with the same standard, but they are moving, talking, excited about learning. Underperforming students need active, thought-provoking learning experiences to grow. Why can't the teachers equipped with these lessons be assigned to the learners who need them the most? In high schools, teachers who have earned their stripes often want to teach AP and honors classes. It might have taken years to get those coveted spots teaching highly motivated students.

Principals want to keep those teachers happy—they will say privately that they don't want to risk losing those teachers, so they comply. Often, that means that newer teachers are assigned to overflowing classrooms of freshmen, which is when students begin dropping out. These teachers are typically wonderfully passionate, but they are still learning the craft of teaching, how things work in the building, and how to run the copiers. More experienced teachers have had years to absorb the curriculum and develop effective lessons. Plus, less experienced teachers might be concerned about discipline issues with struggling learners. Ironically, the most common remedy is a teacher-centered, student-sitting framework, which can exacerbate behavior issues.

Human and material resources need to be distributed to ninth grade (and, depending on your data, eighth grade too). One solution in some high schools is that AP/honors teachers each take one section of ninth grade. But beyond scheduling, is there a stigma attached to teaching struggling learners? Do we send kids a message that some students matter more than others? Are we celebrating our core and remedial teachers as well? One district I visited recently found the solution: they hired the perfect fit, a teacher whose passion was changing outcomes in math. This school put all their eggs in one very capable math basket. In another school I visited, all the remedial reading students in ninth grade were assigned to a single teacher; unfortunately, this was a case of putting all the eggs in a poorly constructed instructional basket. At first, I was enthused about the stacks of high-interest books on the shelves. I asked the students, almost all male, "Are these the books you guys have been reading this semester?" Student after student told me, "Oh, we don't do any of the reading—the teacher has read them all to us." These weaker reading students would be faced with the same end-of-course test as the rest. How would they fare? Equally important, perhaps, how would they pass the written portion of their driver's license test, or do their taxes?

WHAT ABOUT ALL THOSE GAPS?

Seeing students' strengths can be difficult when their gaps are so readily visible. By the time some students reach middle and high school, the gaps are often larger, simply because they have covered so much curricular ground. Fractions, apostrophes, parts of speech, probability—the list of skills potentially missed grows with the child. There is an instinctive reaction to return to everything they did not get in prior grades. In fact, some courseware is designed in this futile manner. When students take a preassessment in math, the weakest students go the farthest back—how in the world will they ever catch up? They don't. Even if it takes every ounce of instructional discipline, this backward tactic should be avoided. First, there's just no time to revisit all things past—there's hardly time to teach the current standards, much less something they didn't get in fourth grade. Second, students do not learn well out of context; instead, they need to apply the skills. Third, students need to brush up on just the past skills for the new standards they are learning. All gaps are not equally important. Fourth, struggling students often have a lot of gaps in several subject areas, often due to memory issues. A tactical, forward-moving plan is in order.

Scaffolding is one part of that process and, as mentioned earlier, looks different according to the student and purpose. For English learners, scaffolding may include supports for language acquisition and/or vocabulary. For the ADHD learner, scaffolding may include memory items or supports for structure and organization. For students behind in reading, text may be marked with synonyms for vocabulary, may be shorter in length, or may include more pictures as cues.

For students on the fast track to dropping out, however, scaffolding may be all of the above. Their gaps in prerequisite skills may have caught up with them. To tell students that they should have learned this in a prior grade is counterproductive and unfair to learners. Schools' sequential, age-based system in which place value, for example, is to be mastered by every child at a predetermined point does not address the reality of learners. Scaffolding provides another opportunity to revisit a skill in the context of new learning. Many teachers utilize interactive notebooks, which can also be digital, that include concrete devices, such as a place value chart or list of irregular verbs, so that the students have everything they need to be successful. Saying, "It's been a while since you've worked with surface area, so there's a cheat sheet on your desks," is more productive than, "You should already know this." Even for solid students, the demands on the working memory all day tax many beyond their limits. But for learners in peril, success in class today is compromised without these supports.

Scaffolding, however, does not mean reteaching prior years' standards to the entire class. Rather, it is a judicious, personalized process designed to keep students in the game.

HOW ACCELERATION MIGHT BE JUST THE TICKET TO SUCCESS

Acceleration has many definitions in education. For gifted and talented students, acceleration means advancing the content, or compressing it so that learning moves at a faster pace. For students in academic peril, however, acceleration is a tactical process that strategically jump-starts them ahead of their peers, by providing prior knowledge, vocabulary, and an ounce of remediation in the skills that will be required just for the upcoming concept. Acceleration gets to the underpinnings of why students are struggling in an academic subject. It sets students up for success by providing them with the right academic background knowledge they need to learn today. The goal of acceleration is for students to learn new concepts alongside their peers, rather than being perpetually behind. Acceleration can provide a fresh start for today's learning, rather than only focusing on a laundry list of deficits.

An instructional coach at the time, I began using this process out of frustration over seeing the same students' names on academic deficiency lists. These middle school students, who were all failing multiple subjects, had been through the list of remedial interventions we offered. Some also had behavioral issues, including suspensions. I phoned their parents and explained that I would like to try getting these children ahead a day or two in the content so that when the concepts were introduced by the general education teacher, they would have a core understanding—something upon which to build. I would introduce the concepts they would learn in math and science in the next day or so, but with very hands-on strategies. We began our TIP chart during that time, getting a sneak peek at the academic words they would be seeing. Remedial instruction was only for skills they would need immediately and could apply in class. For example, if fractions were to be used, I explained this to students as a "blast from the past." We would make scaffolding devices to be pulled out as needed. The best part was telling students they would have access to information that their friends had yet to see.

Acceleration can be implemented in many ways. In my first situation, I used tutoring time before and after school. Some schools have the flexibility of an additional class period, which is perfect for acceleration. In one middle school where I consulted, the principal created a zero period in which every student went somewhere. Math was their school focus, so a selected group went to their math teachers' classrooms for around 30 minutes. The teachers introduced the day's concept, began talking about critical vocabulary, and rehearsed the skills needed to be successful on this new concept. The teachers enlisted these students to be leaders later in the day, when their peers would be seeing this information for the first time. An elementary school where I consulted accelerated students at the very end of the day, introducing the next day's concept. Their rationale was that those final minutes of the day were largely being underutilized. And in yet another elementary school, reading acceleration was implemented in a lunch-and-learn format. This group of Montreal educators (Oppedisano & Goffredo, 2017) documented their journey—and the wonderful increases their students realized—in a journal article (in English).

Imagine the potential of setting students up for success by giving them a little prior knowledge of math, science, or reading lessons just in time for new learning. That's what acceleration does. Student motivation increases as their brains shout, "Hey, I know something about this!" In addition, memory, curiosity, reading comprehension, and participation all improve because we are, in essence, supplying what's missing.

The beauty of acceleration is that remediation is provided, but only what students need this week for the current new concept. Students will apply the skills right now because this remediation is in context. The primary focus is on moving forward, not backward. If we are about to study the phases of the moon, for example, students might watch a video or draw the phases. New vocabulary is introduced. If students are going to be studying area and perimeter, the acceleration class might go on a scavenger hunt for examples, read a storybook, or use manipulatives. Students might read a different story from the same author, preview new vocabulary, or engage in an advanced reading as preparation. The acceleration group stays one step ahead of the rest of the class. In contrast to the deficit model of pounding away at the past, students have opportunities to shine in class—to have great days at school. How do we know it's working? The gauge is how they are doing in class today, in direct contrast to whole-scale remediation, which tends to run on a parallel track.

It is tough to find research support for the old remedial model. It's based on a mistaken logic that if we could just plug every hole students have, they'd be just fine. First, there is little connection between students activities during remediation time versus regular class. For example, they might be relearning perfect squares during remediation, but studying symmetry in math class. Students don't realize success in class using that approach. Second, instructional time spent going backward while other students move forward is fails to close gaps. Third, there's a sense of futility as students get older—always being behind their peers takes a toll on them. Last, students (like mine) had large gaps in more than one subject area—trying to revisit all of that was not workable.

Building prior knowledge and vocabulary just in time for new learning gets hands up in the air and pencils moving. It boosts reading comprehension, retention of information, and student motivation. In fact, teachers have expressed concern to me that these remedial kids were now turning into show-offs in class, bragging about all they know. I can live with that.

A good rule of thumb I use is 75% forward, 25% in reverse. Acceleration is not preteaching, which brings tedium. It is a measured approach that tactically places just enough prior knowledge in a student's path in time for new learning. If crustaceans are up next in science, a 10-minute picture book or video with vocabulary introductions might be ample. For circumference, string and jar lids can get the ball rolling.

What students already know is one of the strongest predictors of how they will learn new information in class (Marzano, 2004). And while it works with all students, consider the potential impact for students from economically disadvantaged homes who may not have the academic vocabulary and experiences that other learners have. Acceleration provides just enough, right when they need it.

THE FEEDBACK DILEMMA

The critical role feedback plays in improving student work has been universally established. The trouble with students in the throes of failure is that they may not be working much. And if they are, they might be understandably sensitive about sharing their work. In their minds, the answer on their paper is probably wrong anyway. Observe the difference in student behavior when graded work is returned. High-achieving students often have a different relationship with graded items—they tend to think the grading system is fair and may even enjoy getting graded items back. Yeah! More items to stick on the refrigerator! They often call out, "Can we take a grade on this?" Harlen and Crick (2003) report that high-achieving students are better at taking tests, demonstrate more perseverance during tests, and feel better about them. That makes sense. But what happens when struggling students get graded items back? They often wad them up or ask if they can toss them. They just want to get rid of the evidence. For this group of students, low marks on papers simply confirm their self-perception as academic losers. In addition, they often don't see these grades as a path to improvement but rather, as further evidence of their low value as students.

Grades can serve as a demotivator for low-achieving students, and yet students have to be graded. What works better for this group is a steady stream of nongraded, soft, formative assessments designed for feedback. Feedback can be the most powerful tool in an educator's arsenal. To give feedback that promotes learning, however, depends on first observing student work. In other words, their work is *our* feedback for how the lesson is working for students. This ongoing descriptive, nonevaluative feedback supports learners in reaching targets and moving upward. Ongoing feedback also enables students to learn faster. According to Black and William (1998), students can learn in six or seven months material that would (without feedback) take a year—that's about twice as fast! For students who are behind, picking up speed is essential. A classroom environment in which students receive large amounts of feedback on their work can build confidence for graded pieces. Feedback is particularly impactful for low-achieving students. As they get some positive feedback and steps for improvement, they feel the power of small successes. They get to experience the good feeling that results. Of course, the feedback must be genuine; students, especially older ones, are keenly aware of disingenuous praise, which can even spark further shame.

Frequent formative assessments are particularly critical for low-performing students in order to monitor their progress, to ascertain what's working for them, and to intervene quickly to fix issues. Some students in this situation attempt to hide in class, to conceal their struggles due to embarrassment with peers. I prefer low-stress, novel quick checks that look nothing like quizzes. Many apps are already available that work for soft formative assessments. One issue with some of the apps is that students cannot show their work—they are often all multiple-choice questions. However, these are largely positive and enable teachers to quickly assess what students know and intervene.

But even with all the technology in the world, it's hard to beat a simple sticky note as a formative assessment. In my sessions, here's how I model sticky note formative assessments: "Grab a sticky and put your name on the sticky side. Now, solve this problem [or answer this question]. When you're ready, just splash it up here on the board and let's take a look at it." Gradually, students rise from the desks and splash their stickies. Every student gets some feedback, albeit quickly. It might sound like this: "Totally on the right track, but check that decimal and bring it back." Sometimes, it's just, "Boom!" Or, "You two missed this step right here. Work together to fix it and bring it right back so we can look at it again." Out of thousands of students, I've only seen one who would not engage in a sticky note assessment. A high school student, she wandered around the room clutching her sticky note, clearly worried that her answer might not match the others. Through my lens, however, her behavior provided just the feedback I needed about her progress. For practice time, she was positioned in a group that could provide some support—all based on a sticky note. Since students' names are on the back, the notes get flipped and rearranged for practice groups.

I visited a high school classroom where a masterful teacher used sticky notes in a different way. During their individual practice time, he tactically starred certain problems. When they reached those problems, students put down their papers or screens, solved one problem on a sticky note, and placed it on the board. The teacher visited with the students right then and discussed the work—they remedied any problems and got the go-ahead to continue to the next section. He did not want students to continue practicing the wrong way. However, although sticky notes are very versatile and students love getting out of those desks, when a strategy is overused the impact can diminish. Many teachers have students write on their desks with erasable markers; others use plastic covers on their work and do quick checks. For novelty, I've even filled plastic plates with salt and had students work with cotton swabs and then shake to erase. The possibilities are limitless. But with academically imperiled students, feedback and some encouragement are critical. These novel ideas encourage students to show their work in a safe, ungraded way. Thumbs up, nodding heads, or asking everyone if they've got it are not formative assessments. Students in academic distress are often the last ones to tell you things are not going well and may want to fly below the radar. They will likely give you thumbs up all day long to avoid drawing attention to themselves. Hovering around their desks too much, in addition, can also cause embarrassment. But fun, safe, ungraded formative assessments can play an important role in building confidence and success and prepare them for graded assessments.

FEEDBACK GOES BOTH WAYS

A safe, student-centered environment should include an ongoing structure for students to provide feedback to teachers. After all, it's their learning. Consider what businesses do: they practically hound customers for information about their shopping, dining, or customer service experiences. Please take a short survey, they implore. Businesses know that survival depends on a satisfying experience for the consumer. Learners aren't exactly consumers, but close. Feedback could consist of a question midweek: "I need you guys to write me two lines about what's working well for you in class and what's not." Or "Write down the one thing you think I need to know about how this unit is going and drop it on the box—no name required," or even, "Rate this lesson on a scale of 1 to 5 and tell me one thing I could do better for the next period class." We cannot be afraid to ask students what's not working for them. From how we can teach parts of speech more effectively, to the books we read, to how students are grouped, routinely query students about what how the school can adjust to better serve them.

KEEPING THE CANNED PROGRAMS ON THE SHELF

Education professor Susan Dynarski (2018), in an interesting piece for the *New York Times*, summarizes the research on which students benefit from online courses. For those on the front lines of credit recovery and remedial education, this will not come as a surprise. Academically challenged students do not fare well on self-taught, online courses. Even if they pass the online course, further testing often reveals that they did not retain the material. Students who are already good at the subject, often math, do very well with this approach, sometimes even better than in a course taught by a teacher. Hybrid or blended courses are more effective for students not skilled in a subject. What we know: Struggling students need the support of a good teacher.

The Bronx Arena school is a place for students who have dropped out (or were kicked out) of school. Carr (2017) details how this school was ahead of the curve in understanding the role online courses might play in supporting students to gain needed credits for graduation quickly. These teachers and leaders fixed some of the issues surrounding online courses for academically challenged students, such as an overreliance on multiple choice answers, little critical thinking, and low interest and relatability. Teachers designed classes around the individual needs of students—using the speed of the digital world but keeping their personal support. Their online component is entirely teacher constructed and infuses high-interest aspects, such as scenes from popular television programs. Students read on screens or watch videos and then share work with their teachers, using the benefits of the digital world while maximizing the power of the teacher and personalized learning.

Mauston High School in Wisconsin used canned online programs as a credit recovery solution for 10 years. Educators there sought something different that would authentically engage students and promote interaction with other students and teachers. In addition, they wanted to ramp up rigor and alignment with their standards. This need for change led to an entirely new approach (Tambornino, 2019). They created a teacher-generated, hands-on approach to learning that would help students graduate. Field trips were integrated, such as science trips to the planetarium and a wildlife refuge. (Due to the high poverty rate, these were cost-free.) Students visited the local museum and examined primary and secondary sources in class. Life skills were taught, included how to file taxes, open a bank account, and understand health insurance. Encouraging results include an increase in reading scores of 3.6 years in just seven months and a jump in writing scores.

THE CHANGING TIMES

There was a time when good jobs were available for workers without a high school diploma. Veterans after World War II, for example, returned home and secured jobs that enabled them to provide for their families.

The Center on Education and the Workforce predicted that 65% of the jobs in 2020 will require coursework after high school (Carnevale, Smith, & Strohl, 2014). And while their analysis predicts a shortage of workers in 2020, only 12% of those jobs might be available to those without at least a diploma. By comparison, in 1972, 32% of jobs did not require a diploma. Many of the new jobs will be in STEM and health care fields, which require specialized post–high school training.

High school graduation rates vary significantly among groups of students. Per the U.S. Department of Education (Stark, Noel, & McFarland, 2015), Asian/Pacific Islander students have the lowest dropout rate at 3.3%; whites are about 1% higher. American Indian/Alaska Native students leave school at a very high rate, an alarming 14.6%, and almost 13% of Hispanic students fail to make it to graduation, along with 7.5% of black students. As a group, students without disabilities graduate at much higher rates—in total, almost 92%. Students with disabilities have a significantly lower graduation rate of 81.5%. And, as mentioned in Chapter 2, a staggering 37% of English language learners leave school without graduating.

The dropout numbers also veil the disparity between high- and low-SES students. U.S. Department of Education statistics reveal that the bottom 20% SES have five times higher dropout rates than the top 20% (Chapman, Laird, Ifill, & KewalRamani, 2011). These statistics turn into real children when we look at actual districts. For example, in a very large district in my state, the higher-SES schools in 2018 boasted a graduation rate over 95%, but two of the lower-SES schools only graduated 65% (Brasch, 2018).

The lives of students will likely be much better if they graduate—this is understood. Being a high school graduate, according to Freudenberg and Ruglis (2007), is urgent enough that it could almost be framed as a wonder tonic for better health. In fact, they believe that dropout prevention should be framed as a public health issue. Why? Individuals who possess more education smoke less, enjoy better health, and live longer. High school grads tend to have more control over their lives, better jobs, less substance abuse, better mental health, and less stress.

The connection between dropping out and incarceration has been heavily documented over a long period of time. One study estimates that dropouts are somewhere between two and eight times more likely to be incarcerated than graduates. From a national perspective, the numbers are staggering. Approximately 75% of state prison inmates in the United States dropped out of high school. Incarceration can have a lifetime impact. Jarrett (2018) proposes that being incarcerated—even for a short time—can change one's personality. Many experience lack of trust or even paranoia. Many become more emotionally detached and have more difficulty with impulsivity than before being incarcerated. The lack of intellectual stimulation throughout the long days can reduce ambition. The loss of autonomy and privacy impacts many as well. In sum, once released, these individuals are changed—and often for the worse.

And for those who are reformed and determined to forge a new path, there's a pragmatic realization. A criminal record makes securing any job much more difficult, especially in the day of one-click access for background checks. There is a long list of jobs they cannot even apply for anymore, from firefighting to truck driving to pest control to social work, depending on the locale. Couloute and Koph (2018) estimate the unemployment rate for formerly incarcerated individuals at over 27%. Black women who were incarcerated have an unemployment rate of 43.6%. Finding housing becomes more difficult as well, as rental agencies often check applicant backgrounds. This is a path no one wants for our children. And while so much is out of educators' control, doing everything we can to keep kids in school to graduate can most certainly provide a more optimistic outlook for their lives.

RESEARCH TO PRACTICE

Dropping out is not just a high school problem—that's just where the paperwork is done. Issues relating to a student's decision to leave school despite the bleakest of warnings begin in different places along their journey. Policies with good intentions, like grade-level retention, have inadvertently pushed students out of school. At one time, students left school mostly to get married or join the military. Now, it's largely due to being unsuccessful in their coursework—they are often drowning academically. In addition, many students do not even like school. The changing reasons why students leave has prompted fresh solutions in some districts. A movement away from canned programs toward more interesting and relevant lessons, and an increased focus on freshman issues are just a few. To break the dropout pattern means pushing back against the old practice of giving struggling learners more passive, boring seat work, which can exacerbate the problem. The most innovative instruction we can muster with the most compelling lessons imaginable are what it takes to keep kids engaged in school. In addition, including them in extracurricular activities can pay dividends.

While graduation rates have improved in many districts, the job landscape has changed dramatically, making the urgency even greater. The days of being qualified for a job without a high school diploma have largely vanished. Further commitment to graduating all students is required, so that not one student has to live with the hardships, lack of opportunity, and shame of not being a high school graduate. They may not appear vulnerable at all, and yes, their decisions have certainly contributed to their state. But as the adults in the building, we know what may await them if we don't do everything we can to change that trajectory. Figure 5.1 is a starting point of practices to break the failure cycle.

Figure 5.1: REDUCING FAILURE

PRACTICES SCHOOLS SHOULD INCREASE	PRACTICES SCHOOLS SHOULD DECREASE
Attendance initiatives	Grade-level retention
Behavioral remedies besides suspension	Fees for summer or other credit recovery
Bridge programs for ninth grade	Suspensions for less serious infractions
Scaffolding prerequisite skills	Canned programs
Acceleration for prior knowledge gaps	Passive, tedious work
Frequent ungraded feedback	Exclusion from extracurricular activities
Inclusion in extracurricular activities	Short-straw approach to teacher selection
Ongoing efforts to fix failure	Redoing entire course, rather than only standards missed
Hands-on, engaging learning	

Real-life examples of students who overcame great odds to become highly successful inspire us. Stephen J. Cannell, for example, failed three grades in school. His parents and teachers told him that he simply was not applying himself—he should just study harder. He loved to write, but his spelling was so bad that he only used words that he was certain of. He saw himself as stupid. But Stephen persevered and actually made it to college. A writing professor saw something in him and implored him to use all the words he knew, not just the ones that he could spell correctly. This freedom to write without worry over criticism of his spelling changed his life. Cannell went on to be one of the most prolific television screenwriters in history, writing and producing hit shows like *The Rockford Files* and *The A-Team* and penning 18 novels (Dyslexia Help, 2019).

These stories are exceptional. Unfortunately, a likelier future for students who don't graduate is a life fraught with barriers to their potential: lower-paying jobs, higher unemployment, more health problems, and a greater likelihood of incarceration. At a high school recently, I was drawn to a word splash of sticky notes on a wall. The center one said simply, "Dropout." Around that word, educators' responses filled the wall. Most were the expected expressions, such as "Less Job Opportunities" and "Tragic." But one said, "Let Them Fail." My hope is that this teacher was thinking of building grit or learning how to overcome obstacles. But these are kids, not adults, and may not possess that level of resolve or personal experience. Yes, it can be exhausting teaching them. They are in the throes of failure, and sometimes just the fact that they are still showing up in the place that's the source of failure is a small sign of hope—and even a little courageous on their parts.

QUESTIONS TO PONDER

- Are there push factors in our buildings or districts that warrant reconsideration?
- Could acceleration be implemented at your school?
- Are all students encouraged to participate in extracurricular activities?
- Are credit recovery programs thoughtfully constructed for the needs of students? Are they creating graduates?

- Are the teachers working with students who face academic challenges the best match?
- Is grade-level retention a practice in your school or district? If so, what alternatives can be developed?
- Do students on the verge of dropping out still matter to us...or have we written them off?

MOVING FORWARD

➤ Are all students, even those at the cusp of dropping out, encouraged to participate in extracurricular events? Are there push factors in your school, district, or state that are inadvertently encouraging dropout? What are educators' perceptions of students on the brink of exiting?

_____

_____

_____

_____

_____

_____

CHAPTER 6

Just Marking Time

On the last day of my last class before I began my first teaching job, the professor asked us if there were questions—perhaps things not addressed in class. My determined hand shot up. "What are we to do if we ask students to do something and they refuse?" This was not just my burning question—it was my biggest worry in the middle of the night. I was embarking on a high school position with over 150 students in my charge—how would a young woman who looked a lot like a teenager have any credibility with these students? Would they even do what I asked of them? What were my next steps if they did not comply? How long would I last? What if things spiraled out of my control? What if I got fired? How long would the water department let me ride before making a payment?

The very nice professor became a bit flummoxed, and stammered a bit, but no answer came forth. Fast forward: After teaching a jillion students, working with thousands of teachers in professional development, coaching educators, and being honored to witness fabulous work in countless classrooms, here's what I know: It was the wrong question to ask. Rather than asking about mechanisms to control students—an impossible task—our focus is really: How can we ignite an intrinsic joy in learning that significantly reduces the need to manage, control, or even kick out kids?

It took me two years of teaching to reframe that question. My fear of not being in control of a classroom led me down a path of crafting highly detailed, reactionary discipline plans that I would impose on learners. Rather than beginning with the creation of valuable tasks that would inspire students to work hard, I spent my time crafting contingency plans for every conceivable move they might make and what my counterpunch might be. I wove my assessment plan in there as well—let them rack up some zeroes on homework for a while and see how they loved learning then! My passion to become a great teacher and change the world had been hijacked by my own insecurities and lack of understanding. Ironically, this led to the development of a teacher-centered, passive, joyless classroom. My plan worked well—students didn't move, call out, or share original ideas. I was securely in control, and every minute that passed felt like a stress-filled eternity.

Today, if I'm working in a building and a conversation about classroom management issues ensues, I have learned to look at things through a different lens, because having authentically engaged, motivated, involved students begins with the tasks we have crafted for them. A great lesson doesn't ameliorate every motivation or discipline issue, but, in my experience, it's where we have to start. Rather than examining the effectiveness of classroom management strategies, my attention goes to student motivation.

If students are not engaged in the tasks being undertaken, I first examine the tasks. How are learners responding to the lesson that has been constructed for them? I consider pacing, interest, level of difficulty, the rate at which the teacher turns the most compelling work over to students, peer interactions, the tone in the room. And, yes, many other factors come into play in terms of student behaviors, including worries about home, conflict with peers, lack of sleep, attention issues, trauma, frustration, or even the time of day. However, I always begin by supporting the teacher in developing stellar, student-centered (but structured) learning experiences first. Next, we observe for changes in student responses to the new lesson. By proactively making changes in how the content is taught—for example, making learning more hands-on, relevant, and collaborative— we can authentically engage almost all of the learners in the classroom. Then we can step back and develop solutions for the remaining students experiencing behavioral or nonparticipation issues that necessitate individualized supports.

By starting with lessons first, off-task or disruptive behaviors are typically reduced enough to get a clearer view of our direction. Again, compelling lessons won't fix everything, but the best classroom management system in the world can't repair a poorly constructed lesson.

So, what makes one student work hard and another just sit there?

WHAT MOVES US TO WANT TO LEARN?

Consider the strength it takes for a student who is not doing well at school to continue even showing up. The bus pulls up again to the same place where things didn't go well yesterday. Again, they have to muster the courage to try, in the face of mounting negative evidence. Trying something new requires taking a chance on failing. So, what motivates students to work hard, anyway? What pieces put into play can move them to be successful?

When I was a 19-year-old college student, I took a swimming class for one of my physical education credits. In that class was an older, foreign student who spoke just a little English. He was terrified of the water. On the first day of class, our coach encouraged and coaxed him to sit on the edge of the pool and simply dangle his feet. (The rest of us just jumped in.) The next day, the student sat on the upper steps of the pool and splashed around. Later, he trusted the coach enough to clutch the teacher's neck and venture out a few feet and then return to the safety of the steps. A week into class, we witnessed this thirtyish man finally place his face in the water. By the end of the summer session, he was able to jump in the pool from the side and swim the width of the pool. His "final exam" was greeted with thunderous applause by the rest of the class—a bunch of college kids who'd grown up around swimming pools.

What would possess a grown man who feared even putting his face in the water to take an optional swimming class? He could have chosen soccer, tennis, ballroom dance, badminton—you name it—but he selected swimming, a sport in which his personal self-efficacy was categorically bleak. The logical conclusion, for those of us who witnessed it: being able to swim was so hugely valuable to him that he was willing to risk it all—embarrassment, indignity, and potential failure. He left that class a swimmer.

What we observed was a cornerstone of motivation in action: the perception of the task as personally valuable was worth risking failure. Plus, the student made the choice to take on this particular task, another factor of motivation. In addition, the swimming coach made all the right motivational moves. Goals were appropriate in difficulty, there was ample modeling, feedback was ongoing and descriptive, and progress was evident.

THE MOTIVATED CLASSROOM

Extrinsic motivation includes stickers, candy, points, and pizza parties. Before long, students are apt to do just the minimum to earn the prize. As they get older, the prize package becomes more grandiose—perhaps some lakefront property—or it's not worth earning. Truly motivated learners work hard for the satisfaction of an accomplishment, the pride of a job well done. A nod from their favorite teacher makes their week—or perhaps they work hard not to let their team down. So what makes one student jump in and work hard and another just sit idly by? How is it that one teacher's class will see every student authentically involved—and right next door there's a different situation? What motivates an individual to want to work hard and strive for higher levels is understandably complex. Three elements (and there are others) of focus to improve motivation are:

- Self-efficacy
- The value of the task and how it's designed (lessons)
- Classroom and school environment

CAN I EVEN DO THIS?

Students who have experienced failure are understandably reluctant to jump into a math, reading or science pool. Failure hurts; shame hurts. Self-efficacy, Bandura (1984) explains, is an individual's own judgment about his or her chances of performing at a certain level. As we are busy instructing, our students' brains are making quick assessments of their personal propensity for success, whether they are more likely to experience success or failure at the impending task. How much is each student willing to risk on this task? For example, pretend that the tasks below are being announced in class. Rate your own self-efficacy about how success-ful you'll likely be (1 is low; 5 is high).

___ Make five basketball layup shots in a row
___ Play the lead role in a musical
___ Multiply fractions on a timed test
___ Run a test on water quality

On which tasks did you feel strongly about your chances for suc-cess? Which ones would you prefer not doing at all? Self-efficacy goes up and down. In some areas, our past experiences—both successes and failures—signal green lights. Yet, in others, we practically break out in a cold sweat at the thought of engaging in the task. The good news about student self-efficacy is that learners tend to work harder, persevere longer, and participate more readily in a task of high confidence (Schunk & Meese, 2006). In addition, a high level of self-efficacy results in more achievement, as well as a greater likelihood of overcoming obstacles Usher & Pajares, 2008). More optimistic, less anxious learners tend to have higher self-efficacy.

The flip side is also true. Students who view themselves as incapable academically tend to give up quickly at a task—or avoid it completely (Brophy, 2010). Unlike their classmates with high self-efficacy, these stu-dents are more pessimistic and stressed out (Pajares, 2006). In class, this may resemble a failure cycle: their plummeting academic self-perception can lead to shutting down in class—avoiding that which brings more of the same feeling of being a failure. If our response is to assign them reme-dial-type, tedious work, their motivation may decline further. Why? Their low personal self-efficacy is now combined with tedious, demotivational work. Educators and leaders may implore these students to work harder. Others just leave them alone. The optimism they once had for academic successes has dimmed.

The good news is that self-efficacy is not fixed on a line—it can move upward. But doing that takes more than telling learners, "You can do it!" They need to realize small successes again—because success can increase the desire for more success. Research shows that as students start gaining proficiency in a task, their self-efficacy starts to rise, and the more frequent the success, the higher the self-efficacy (Zimmerman & Cleary, 2006). What healthy self-efficacy looks like in classrooms: participation, work ethic, and sustained effort. These successes can create an upward spiral. These students also need to become a part of the class again, because failure can be isolating.

Here are the strategies that I employ in schools to spark and maintain (or rebuild) learner self-efficacy:

- Begin the learning episode with something powerfully compelling that is not graded. Examples: something from the science news to debate, a real-world problem, an agree/disagree sort with a partner, a riveting quick write, an error analysis, or a lab activity. Opening a unit on lab safety? Students can read about Marie Curie and identify lab safety issues from her time. About to teach juvenile justice? Consider beginning with news articles from the community involving juvenile issues. They get students participating right away and provide an authentic avenue to commend them for their thinking, responses, and so on. The opposite of this practice is bland warm-ups or going over homework—which failing kids probably can't even find.
- Incorporate choices throughout the lesson. Choices move some of the control onto students' shoulders. Students who are underperforming at school may feel that many things are outside their sphere of control. By making decisions about their job to do in a group, how to demonstrate their understanding of a topic, picking which reading strategy works best for them, or what technology to use, students feel more intrinsically motivated to participate.
- Make it hands-on. Incorporate sorts, drawing, math manipulatives, construction, labs, video creation, and so on, to encourage action.
- Incorporate quick, descriptive, ongoing feedback. However, feedback isn't always the teacher talking to the student. An answer key positioned three feet away is feedback, or even a teacher-made video explaining the answers. Elbow partners or groups can provide feedback. Students can self-assess by highlighting a strength and an area of concern. In addition, empower students to provide feedback to teachers. Feedback loops rely on visual observation from the start of class to the close. The work students are producing is the cornerstone of the feedback.

- Set proximal goals and join students in checking them off. This might look like a checklist or agenda outlining today's lesson. In addition, support students in setting goals. For example, if the class is working on crafting introductory paragraphs, you could break it down into three parts: (1) write a captivating opening statement; (2) preview what's coming; and (3) create a transition.
- Incorporate acceleration to provide prior knowledge and scaffolding just in time for new learning. This enables underperforming students to gain inside information about what will be learned in the next session, to shore up just the prerequisite skills and critical vocabulary for the next couple of lessons.
- Pair and group students with a thoughtful purpose. Pairing a struggling physics student with Einstein will yield predictable results: Einstein will answer the problem in two seconds without scratch paper and then all work stops. The other partner just nods and says, "Yep, that's the answer I got as well." Grouping students effectively depends on the task, student strengths, and social dynamics. Each student should have an authentic, typically separate role to play, as well as opportunities for leadership. One student might be a dynamo at organization, another at keyboarding, and yet another at drawing. Some are fast readers; others love exploring new technology.
- Utilize frequent, nongraded quick checks.

Interestingly, teacher self-efficacy plays an important role in student motivation as well. Hoy and Davis (2006) describe teacher self-efficacy as our own judgment about our abilities to impact student learning and engagement, even among students we find to be unmotivated or even difficult. For example, some teachers might perceive themselves as highly capable of teaching honors students but less confident about how they might do in remedial math. But teachers who are highly self-efficacious can work wonders with lower-achieving students; in fact, their classes often experience better student outcomes and learner motivation. They are often more organized and enthusiastic, and expend more of their talents on constructing meaningful lessons. Self-efficacious teachers lecture less and are more apt to utilize inquiry-based learning and incorporate small groups into learning. These gems are less critical of student errors, work harder and longer with struggling students, and are less controlling on discipline.

Conversely, a teacher with low confidence in the area of classroom management, especially beginning teachers, may avoid the exact strategies that will motivate students, such as hands-on science labs. And teacher self-efficacy extends to the formation of student relationships as well, a critical need for students. Teachers need to feel comfortable with students of all academic situations and backgrounds, including those with a history of behavioral issues in class (Hoy & Davis, 2006). Educators who are the best match for lower-performing students are self-efficacious, comfortable with their content, open to all kinds of kids and what they bring to the classroom and possess a deep tool kit of evidence-based practices.

TASKS AND MOTIVATION

In a three-year study by Hansen (1989), the behaviors of students were examined as they related to various tasks. When students perceived tasks as personally valuable and believed they could be successful, they engaged in the lesson. Makes sense. But what's interesting is that even when their self-efficacy was high—they knew they could do it—if the task had low value, they evaded the lesson. They saw no reason to even do the task. They would sit and talk or simply go through the motions. For example, copying definitions or information on a slide is something every student can do, but motivation will be low. In the study, when the value of the task was high—something students really wanted to partake in—but self-efficacy was low, students tended to pretend to understand or make excuses. It's important for tasks to be of the appropriate difficulty. Tasks can be chunked or scaffolded to support learners. Questions to determine student motivation: Can I do this? Is there enough value in this task for me to expend a lot of effort? Is this task worth the risk of failure? (Is learning to swim important enough for me to risk drowning?)

Tasks need to be relevant, valuable, and of the appropriate degree of difficulty. Students also need at least a little background knowledge. Learners expend more effort and pay greater attention to tasks for which they already have some underpinning of knowledge (Hattie & Yates, 2014). When learners know a little about something, they tend to want to know more and are more invested in the task. This is why the opening minutes of class are perfect for tapping into prior knowledge and why acceleration can work very well. And while student motivation looks like increased engagement, the way tasks are designed influences memory as well. Willis (2006) contends that memory storage is more effective when students can link to prior knowledge and when a task is personally meaningful. In addition, she shares that when tasks employ more senses, more brain connections are made, which can result in easier recall of information later. Bailey and Pransky (2014) hold that every task should incorporate at least two learning channels to enhance memory. Relevant, valuable, hands-on, multisensory tasks absolutely enhance student motivation and learning.

As mentioned in Chapter 5, current research brings into question an overreliance on canned computer programs for struggling learners. (Blended courses work better.) Recently, I observed a fifth grade classroom in which students who were struggling in math were on computer screens for 50 straight minutes in an attempt to increase low math scores. At the debriefing, I inquired about the possibility of incorporating math manipulatives so that students could explore the concepts with their hands. "We tried that, but students kept playing with them." The use of screens, in my view, may yield short-term results, but students may grow to resist math, an area in which many already experience low self-efficacy. Their high school, which was posting stellar scores, was the opposite: high-volume, hands-on, relevant tasks. Courseware can help, but it can't supplant great teaching.

TURNING STANDARDS INTO COMPELLING TASKS

An overarching consideration in creating dynamic, student-centered tasks is what type and how much explicit teaching is required versus what students can explore and do themselves. For example, in a lesson on the historical period of Reconstruction, the teacher might explicitly teach about complex postwar challenges, such as the currency collapse in the South, the catastrophic number of casualties, and the massive infrastructure damage. Pictures might accompany this, to provide context and prior knowledge. Then students will be equipped with adequate background knowledge to study the historical plans on the table for moving the country forward and to defend the positions they develop. These careful decisions give students opportunities to engage in the richest part of the content.

There are endless ways to create tasks that are riveting and relevant, such as:

- Transform a standard into a problem-solving task.
- Incorporate local interest and news.
- Transform a standard into a situation in which students must defend a position.
- Utilize impactful text, such as real-world success stories (Serena Williams, for example, is the richest self-made woman in the world, and Rihanna's cosmetics company pulled in $570 in revenue in 2019, per Forbes, June 30).
- Game it up. Using PowerPoint, create clues. Provide students with answer cards with the correct responses (examples: angles, figurative language, types of sentences). Click and play!
- Provide choices in tasks and in reading.
- Incorporate labs and other hands-on experiences.
- Incorporate novelty, such as building something out of Legos and then writing about your construction.

For example, if federalism is being introduced, students might first be assigned this short task: On chart paper with your group, list every example of government functions you know about. For example, if someone in your family is getting married, they had to get a marriage license. Perhaps a neighbor just received a traffic ticket. After a few minutes, have them stop. Now, label each of your responses with your best guess about which level of government it belongs to: city, county, state, or federal? Even if their responses are not completely accurate yet, students will see that there are different levels of government. What we about to study is this: Who's got the power? After a short mini lesson for background knowledge, the work can largely be turned over to students. At the end of class, they can revisit their opening task: What changes should be made?

Math offers an array of strategies that pull students in, beyond simply practice problems. Math is all around students, from choices on Netflix to the cafeteria to the angles on the baseball field. Problems can be personalized with students' homes, hobbies, or video games. Many teachers have students insert their own names into stock word problems. In addition to personalizing problems, there are strategies that get students talking, even debating, about math. Agree/disagree is a strategy in which students explain their reasoning, such as in these two statements:

- The median is the only measure that can be determined from a dot plot.
- A histogram can be used to find exact values like the mean.

For the same concept, students can engage in a higher-order thinking strategy called Sometimes, Never, or Always. In pairs or groups, students dig deep to argue whether a statement is always, never, or sometimes true. For example:

- Extreme values affect the mean.
- A data set can have only one median.
- The mean is the middle number in an ordered data set.

Of course, these two strategies can also be utilized in other subjects, from scientific principles to grammar rules.

All students enjoy sorting. Its tactile, ungraded nature adds a game-like dimension. Plus, the multisensory approach strengths retention of information. In the sort shown in Figure 6.1, students arrange the numbers and arrows to show the relationship between the digits. The sort is correctly solved here, but students love figuring out how the pieces go together. In class, these are cut, placed in baggies, and used as stations. Having said that, there's no reason that they could not serve as a quick formative assessment.

And while the one shown is for math, sorts are captivating in all subjects. They can encompass vocabulary, steps in a process, sequencing, or comparing and contrasting. In language arts, students can match types of figurative language with pictures. In science, two columns can be created for invertebrates and vertebrates. In social studies, leaders, movements, and types of economies are examples. In math, students can sequence pictures of fractions from smallest to largest, match fractions to decimals, or differentiate rational from irrational. Sorts are ideal for stations and small groups.

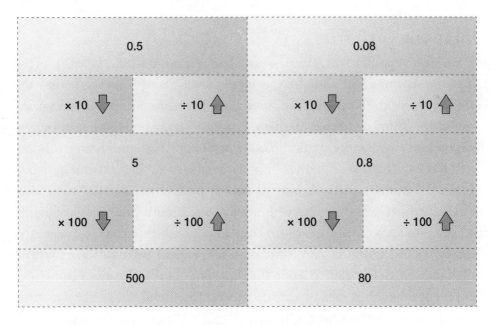

Figure 6.1: PLACE VALUE SORT (SOLVED CORRECTLY)
Source: Used with permission of Math in the Fast Lane (https://www.MathinFastLane
.com).

ENVIRONMENT AND MOTIVATION

A captivating lesson combined with high student self-efficacy is a key pillar of motivation. But students must feel welcomed, relaxed, and safe in their classroom and school environment as well. For some students, school is the safest place they go. Whatever tumult is occurring outside our walls, school offers a place of sanctuary in which adults model civility and a calm, respectful predictability. Schools are fascinating places. Students come from different neighborhoods, economic and cultural backgrounds, and home situations—as do teachers. We merge together into a classroom to learn and work together. From that perspective, one can make the case that things typically go pretty well. But students are not just mastering content; they are learning ways to handle conflict, interact with others, manage stress, and solve problems. The student-centered classroom offers ongoing opportunities for supporting students in these efforts, because, for the bulk of class, teachers are in the midst of students learning with them, not positioned at the front of the classroom.

WHAT'S UP WITH THAT KID?

In 1998, a research team (Felitti et al., 1998) released what's often referred to as the Adverse Childhood Experiences (ACE) Study. He worked as the chief of preventative medicine for Kaiser Permanente in San Diego. As part of the study, a questionnaire was sent to thousands of patients. The respondents were largely middle class, well educated, and had insurance with Kaiser. The researchers sought to discover the relationship between childhood trauma and subsequent health problems. The sheer number of reports of trauma surprised the team, with more than half reporting at least one area of trauma. More than one-fourth reported two or more. The types of trauma were physical, psychological, sexual, living with a substance abuser, violence against a mother, a family member in prison, and mental health issues or suicide of a family member. The team cross-referenced these responses with health records. They discovered a strong relationship between trauma and health problems, including heart disease, cancer, and lung and liver disease. Those with four or more areas of trauma experienced between a 4- and 12-fold increase in alcoholism, drug abuse, depression, and suicide attempts. The higher the ACE score, the greater the association with disease. In addition, childhood trauma victims, the study reported, also experience increased illicit drug use, a much higher number of sexual partners, and more sexually transmitted diseases.

Educators need to be aware of the signs of childhood trauma, its impact on learning and behavior, and tools to support these students. Bessel van der Kolk (2014) has spent much of his lifetime helping trauma survivors. He shares that, as much as trauma survivors would love to move on, the brain does not forget and is forever altered by the experiences. The part of our brain that is used for survival reactivates when it senses even a hint of danger. Trauma victims are hypervigilant to perceived threats; their sense of risk and feeling safe has been forever changed. They react to subtle threats that those without trauma may not even perceive. The brain circuitry sets off an alarm system to protect itself. Stress hormones are released. When sensing danger, their first step is typically to call for help, but it may be with facial expressions rather than words. If no one comes to their rescue, the next step is fight or flight. In the school setting, this is where fists fly or a student bolts out of the room. If flight or fight is not possible, the last phase is to freeze or collapse. The body shuts down to preserve itself and utilize as little energy as possible (van der Kolk, 2015).

The large numbers of learners who have experienced trauma combined with the negative impact of trauma on a child's ability to learn are important to understand. Their unexpected behaviors can mystify the most experienced educator. Once a trauma victim's brain has sounded an alarm of potential danger and the person is on high alert scanning for danger, the primitive survival part of the brain takes over. This partially closes off the higher, rational, cognitive part of the brain. Students' brains are totally focused on survival, and the need to escape or fight their way out becomes paramount. Once they have escaped this perceived danger, their equilibrium and relative calm return (van der Kolk, 2015). But they may have created havoc in their path.

Every educator can recount baffling incidents that match this pattern. On one of my scheduled, formal observations, the administrator came in and chose a seat next to a student who was always well behaved. I breathed a sigh of relief, thinking how well this was going to go for me. But the presence of the assistant principal sitting close by, jotting down notes on her clipboard, somehow unnerved the student. The student became agitated and restless. Rather than check on her, I pushed on, probably because I was so focused on the observation. The eighth grader stood up, yelled at everyone, and flipped her desk over. Papers scattered everywhere, and other students jumped up to dodge flying school supplies—and a desk. She bolted out of the room. To the administrator's credit, she quietly said, "Let's do this another time."

Not all trauma survivors demonstrate hypervigilant fight or flight behaviors. Some children dissociate, which Jennings (2019) describes as a self-protection strategy that provides escape from the pain. In class, dissociation may look like spacing out or attention lapses. In addition, students may expend energy evaluating the teacher's mood, rather than focusing on content. Or they may experience difficulty expressing themselves accurately due to their state of anxiety. Often they have difficulty in social situations and difficulty connecting to peers.

To demonstrate how trauma victims and nonvictims perceive danger differently, van der Kolk and a colleague created a series of picture cards, cut at random from magazines, including innocent scenes of families and communities. They showed these cards to two groups of children, one without traumatic experiences and another that had experienced significant trauma, and asked the children to make up stories to go with the images. Children without trauma made up stories that accurately represented the benign images. For example, they told happy tales about the dad and kids in the picture having lunch together. But the group with trauma saw danger and violence at every turn. Stories of gruesome acts with smashed skulls and blood were created for the same innocent pictures. These were children who had endured horrible trauma, such as seeing a family member murdered or suffering horrible physical abuse. Their worldview had been terribly altered by events in their lives (van der Kolk, 2015).

The distress that trauma survivors revisit again and again is reflected in brain scans and in their physiological responses. In one study, victims and researchers collaborated on two scripts. One script depicted something in their normal routine that was calm and orderly. The second script revisited a traumatic event in their lives, such as a horrific car wreck or parental abuse. As victims read the routine script, normal breathing and heart rates remained, but the script recounting the trauma brought increased heart rates, shallow breathing, and a jump in blood pressure. Brain scans of traumatized subjects revealed a large red spot in the limbic area of the brain called the amygdala, which warns the person of danger and sets off the body's responses to this alert. Stress hormones flood the body to prepare for the impending battle. In these subjects, trauma that had occurred years before was still real enough to trigger the body to respond, almost as if the trauma was happening now. Two individuals who experience the same traumatic event together may demonstrate very different responses. One person's brain lit up, as if he were experiencing trauma in real time. The other person's brain essentially went blank, showing decreased activity, indicating dissociation (van der Kolk, 2014).

The research on the large number of students who have experienced trauma and its lasting repercussions provides educators with some answers about concerning behaviors in the classroom. This knowledge enables meaningful opportunities to provide safe learning environments for all students, and to additionally support specific students in need of concrete plans to gain control and balance in their lives. How can they learn effectively when they are knotted up with anxiety about what they perceive as looming dangers in situations others deem benign? One challenge is that, as educators, we cannot be aware of every student's situation. When I worked in schools with large transient populations, it was routine to get new students every week with little information about them. But even without that dynamic, a secondary teacher might engage with 160 students per day, a coach with an even larger number. Even with those challenges, however, educators can be versed in recognizing behaviors and collaborating on strategies to support these students.

TIPS FOR CREATING A SAFE ENVIRONMENT

In the same way that there are highly effective practices for instruction, there are time-tested principles for creating a positive, safe learning environment for all students. When they are combined with evidence-based instructional practices, students can be relaxed in class and focused on learning. For some students, however, additional strategies will be needed. Here are some considerations for creating positive learning environments for all students:

- The term "expectations" rather than "rules" is now used in many buildings. The reasoning is beyond semantics: some students face dire consequences for breaking rules at home, so the word might seem more negative than intended. In addition, for students seeking to exert control, a rule may feel like something to rebel against. Conversations with students about expectations can be valuable, so that the expectations are not simply imposed on them. They should be framed positively, as ways to be successful and work together, and modeled frequently.
- Avoid practices that bring shame or embarrassment. I frequently see teachers requiring students to publicly move a marker, such as a clip, to a written consequence, such as loss of a privilege. A better practice includes private conversations about behavior that include more positive steps.
- Provide opportunities for students to exercise autonomy. For example, you could allow students to have some say about seating, organizing

materials, whether to stand or sit to work, or partner selection. Students, like teachers, need to feel in control.

- Model that mistakes are part of learning. "Gosh, I made a little calculation error there, didn't I? Thanks for catching that!"
- Get to know students' interests and promote conversations about them, be it movies, baseball, or skateboarding.
- Encourage movement. Read the room and have everyone take a stretch break. Better yet, build movement into lessons.
- Model stress reduction. For example, you could use a computer breathing application and invite students to do some deep breathing with you or have stress balls on hand.
- Monitor the volume of voices in the classroom, including your own.
- Model the civility that we expect of our children.
- Provide a fresh start for students who had a rough day previously. They are understandably nervous about coming back to class.
- Create lessons utilizing teams so that students learn the joy of working together. In addition to content knowledge, students build relationships that provide a support system and increase resilience in them (Jennings, 2019).
- Avoid ultimatums that may create power struggles and may be interpreted as threats.

A benefit of the research on the damage that trauma has inflicted on some of our students is that logic and reason can now be applied to some of the often largely misunderstood incidents in our classrooms. Understanding why they might overreact or respond to certain situations is helpful. We can thoughtfully examine factors that increase the probability of outbursts (or shutdowns) and work with students to create more productive action plans for similar situations. From a certain vantage point, the research can help us predict the behaviors that can upset them, their classmates, and us. Armed with this information, we can better support students so that they are not banished to in-school suspension or worse, suspension and expulsion. It is also vital to recognize that other students in distress have no outbursts at all; they just disappear in class. They may quietly turn in their work (or not), rarely speak, and seem to be no trouble to anyone.

Even in an effective, positive classroom environment, there are students who benefit from additional techniques. Some can be woven into the classroom setting, while others might work well with the school counselor or after school. Additional practices to consider:

- Mindfulness techniques to help students focus on the present, not the past (many schools now utilize these for all students).
- Yoga.
- Improvisation exercises (van der Kolk, 2014).
- Breathing exercises (van der Kolk, 2014).
- An individualized action plan for some students, including steps such as these: (1) breathe deeply; (2) jot down two positive thoughts or read a few pages in your library book; (3) signal for help; and (4) increase movement.
- An opportunity room at school where students can go to gather their composure or visit with a counselor or other advisor.

UNINTENDED CONSEQUENCES: ZERO TOLERANCE

The phrase "zero tolerance" relates to a no-nonsense approach to handling disciplinary infractions by students, including severe punishments for behaviors that are designed to be equally applied across the board, with little allowance for individual circumstances or alternative paths for redemption. Some trace the practice back to the 1980s no-nonsense War on Drugs as a school version of getting tough on rule breakers. Others cite efforts by the federal government in the mid-1990s to mandate lengthy expulsion for any student found with a weapon. The intent of these policies was to make schools safer, largely to keep weapons and drugs out of schools, clearly a worthy mission. Suspensions and expulsions were for egregious infractions. But zero tolerance policies gradually expanded to student behaviors unrelated to drugs or guns into more typical kid behaviors. Suspensions under zero tolerance policies increased significantly, as more infractions fell under this umbrella. Though it's designed to make schools safer places with equal punishment for all, has the zero tolerance approach fulfilled its mission?

Everyone wants safe, orderly schools with a positive atmosphere for learning. A task force examining the effects of zero tolerance policies was assembled by the American Psychological Association (APA). Their report indicates a negative relation between high suspension and expulsion rates and academic achievement, even when adjusting for SES (Skiba et al., 2006). Furthermore, schools with high suspension and expulsion rates tend to have lower satisfaction with school climate, and increased time spent on discipline matters. Plus, the suspensions and expulsions did not appear to prevent future behavioral infractions; instead, incidents among those suspended increased. One of the purported advantages of zero tolerance policies was that all students would receive equal treatment. The evidence, however, reveals that African American students are suspended or expelled at a disproportionate rate and receive more serious punishments than other groups, despite no evidence that their behaviors warranted it. The U.S. Department of Education (2019) reports that in school year 2012, black students were suspended three times more often than whites, and students with disabilities were twice as likely to be suspended.

Another concern cited by the APA task force is the large increase in referrals to the juvenile justice system for more severe infractions (Skiba et al., 2006). They cite the addition of school resource officers and increased surveillance technology as potential factors in this upsurge—incidents that traditionally would have been handled at school are more frequently being referred to juvenile justice. This transfer of responsibility for developing solutions for behavioral infractions to the juvenile justice system—criminalizing the process—has been tagged the school-to-prison pipeline (Skiba et al., 2006). Gonzales (2012) also contends that some schools are using the juvenile justice system to handle school discipline problems. The merging of school and law enforcement in buildings has resulted in more students being referred to juvenile courts for often minor behavioral infractions—incidents that formerly would have been handled by school administrators. Further, she holds that schoolchildren are more policed now than anyone outside of jail, and that the often-severe punishments handed out for things like tardiness and classroom disruptions are pushing students out of school.

A study by Buccanfuso and Kuhfield (2011) mirrors some of the same concerns, namely the expansion of zero tolerance policies into behaviors beyond the original intent of school safety, and that the majority of suspensions today are for nonviolent infractions. They cite an urban school district in which students were suspended for poor attendance, insubordination, and classroom disruptions. The authors bemoan the fact that while zero tolerance initiatives are widespread, scant evidence supports their effectiveness. They recommend nonpunitive approaches that teach students how to resolve conflicts, manage emotions, and improve social skills.

One of the unintended impacts of zero tolerance policies is to increase suspensions at the same time schools are working on increasing attendance rates. Suspensions and attendance are key indicators of future dropout, something many schools track. Academic achievement suffers with suspensions, as students are sent home and are not participating in lessons. It has been accepted for many years that attendance, behavior, and course failures, which we might call the ABCs of dropout, are predictors of future dropout. Suspensions and expulsions impact all three of those predictors. In addition, it is understood that students who drop out are at significantly increased risk for incarceration. In school year 2012 alone, the U.S. Department of Education (2019) reported that 3.45 million students were suspended out of school and 3.5 million were suspended in school, out of 49 million total students.

The overreliance on suspension as a tool to manage student behaviors led Jim Sporleder, a Washington state high school principal, to try something new. Stevens (2012) details how now, when students erupt in class, he sits down with them and talks to them about their stress, anger, and why things just went so wrong in class. He has been startled at how kindness to his students, rather than just booting them out of school, has changed things. He shares that students' defenses tend to break down as they open up about what's happening at home or school. There are still consequences for the behaviors, but they are more likely to be in-school suspension with an attending teacher who is prepared to discuss more effective strategies for handling stressful situations. This new approach by a seasoned administrator has yielded impressive results in drastically cutting out-of-school suspensions, expulsions, and office referrals.

Some schools are pursuing the path of restorative justice. A principle of this framework is that rather than exiling students from school, the school community works together to help the student repair the harm that he or she has inflicted. There are different models of school restorative justice, but, commonly, those who were harmed by the actions—teachers, students, parents, administrators—conference together with the individual who inflicted the damage to develop a resolution. Restorative justice is a cultural and mind-set shift from traditional discipline codes in schools. Advocates allow, however, that schools are different than the larger community in that the person who was harmed will see the individual who inflicted the damage at school again. Supporters of this approach maintain that some of its strengths lie in having students accept responsibility for their actions while creating a positive school culture and reducing suspension rates. Districts and schools have implemented restorative justice in different ways with varying outcomes and degrees of success (Gonzales, 2012). A thorough look at models and results is available here: http://www.ibarji.org/docs/gonzales.pdf.

As the disappointing results of zero tolerance practices have emerged, along with the unintended consequences, educators are seeking alternatives to suspension to improve student behaviors. Here are a few suggestions for strategies instead of suspension (Petersen, 2005):

- Restitution: for example, students wash lockers or repair damage to the school.
- Mini class on more positive behaviors, such as an online course, workbook, or videos.
- Problem-solving with students on more productive behaviors.
- Counseling (counselors in a school where I worked spent a couple of hours each day in In School Suspension [ISS] with students).
- Community service (one principal with whom I worked joined students in ISS in making sandwiches for the local homeless shelter).

RESEARCH TO PRACTICE

Instruction, classroom environment, and student behaviors are intricately interwoven. Captivating, relevant lessons combined with a sense of community have a way of bringing students onboard and keeping them on task. When a high degree of self-efficacy is present and the tasks in front of them have high value, students are not just willing to work, they enjoy it. A well-designed, properly paced learning experience has the power to keep most students authentically engaged, while allowing for additional attention for the few who are not. Success is a motivator. But a tedious, disjointed lesson, most educators will attest, can be a recipe for off-task or disruptive behaviors. Classroom management plans cannot repair an ill-conceived lesson.

Stellar instructional practices have the power to minimize classroom incidents and provide opportunities to focus on students who need additional attention. Students bring their home lives and experiences to school with them. They make mistakes. They blow up unexpectedly. They get their feelings hurt or become embarrassed by things we don't understand. And while educators cannot know all that is going on in students' lives, an understanding of the behaviors often exhibited by trauma survivors helps us seek proactive solutions. These insights can help educators avoid overreacting to the behaviors or taking them personally. A nurturing, relaxed classroom and school environment supports all students in learning.

But we can't teach or inspire kids who are not even present due to suspension. Zero tolerance policies, though well intended in their origin, have damaged students and communities, with meager evidence to support any increase in safety or achievement. And while some students certainly must be suspended, the consensus is that alternative paths will better serve students, schools, and communities. The school community can work with children on more appropriate ways to manage their emotions, make better decisions, and make amends for their infractions.

Once, outside a classroom, I was drawn to some posted student writings. Students were asked for their views on why fourth grade is awesome. And while some opined about recess and lunch, one student wrote, "They always give you a second chance. They're always there for you when you're down." What a mission statement.

QUESTIONS TO PONDER

- What examples of student autonomy can be found in your classroom?
- What examples of student self-efficacy have you seen in your classroom?
- Have you advocated for a suspension, partly due to the lack of feasible alternative paths? (I have...)
- Have you realized in the middle of a fabulous lesson how well students were behaving?

- Have you seen student behaviors becoming problematic during a poorly constructed lesson?
- How comfortable are you in teaching lower-performing students with behavioral challenges?
- On a scale of 1–10, how open are you to pursuing alternatives to suspension?
- In your view, what types of infractions warrant suspension?

MOVING FORWARD

➤ What are three things to try that would increase student motivation and positive behaviors? _____
_____
_____
_____
_____

CHAPTER 7

Final Thoughts

The success (and failures) of students inside the walls of our classrooms can have long-term impacts on students. Job opportunities, mental health, substance abuse, future income, and a dependence on government assistance are frequently connected to how successful students were in school. Interactions between administrators and students in hallways, decisions made in meetings to thwart academic failure at every turn, and coaches encouraging students to join teams—these efforts matter. This is not to say that everything is on educators' already laden shoulders. What this does say, however, is how incredibly important educators are to the lives of children.

Working with vulnerable, underperforming learners requires not just innovative teaching, but a mindset open to giving them a fresh start every day. And while the academic deficits are often apparent, their strengths must be realized and developed. Because simply hammering on deficits all day can take a toll on them; indeed, it can diminish any joy of learning.

And while the case can be made that every student is vulnerable at times, this book has highlighted groups that are underperforming as a whole. In researching each group separately, positive patterns emerged. In every group—from ADHD learners to gifted to ELLs—the critical importance of pulling them into the school community was revealed. Makes sense. When things are not going well at school, the understandable tendency might be to withdraw from school-related activities. Sports and clubs can promote a positive attitude about school. Question: At your school, are there policies in effect that keep struggling learners out of these opportunities? By not including all students in these opportunities to make positive connections, are we exacerbating failure?

The critical nature of prior knowledge as a cornerstone for learning has been understood for many years. Establishing a base of prior knowledge via acceleration is a path some schools are exploring. This practice tactically situates prior knowledge for some students just in time for new learning. The mission is to enable students to effectively learn new information alongside their peers, rather than always be behind. Acceleration time might be during tutoring, a lunch and learn, or even a station during class. In addition, relevant, high-interest lessons increase motivation for all learners, but particularly vulnerable ones. The combination of acceleration prior to powerful learning experiences can be a game-changer for students. These instructional practices are in direct contrast to assigning tedious work to struggling learners.

For all learners, but especially our ELL and lower readers, vocabulary development should be an everyday, ongoing instructional practice. But learning vocabulary is not about long word lists and copying definitions. Vocabulary is learned over time through multiple, different exposures. Throughout my own classroom teaching, my books, and my trainings, I model TIP (Term-Info-Picture) charts. This approach utilizes everyday language, pictures, and multiple exposures. This is built throughout the unit, not preconstructed, and remains on the wall as a reference. But the TIP chart is just one component. Vocabulary understanding is a journey over time. One day, students might compare and contrast two words and the next day they might act out the words. By the end of the week, students might figure out which words fit into a paragraph.

Scaffolding should be a mainstay of working with academically vulnerable learners. But scaffolding is differentiated by the needs of learners. Most of scaffolding, I have witnessed, can be proactively created. After creating a map of the upcoming unit, jot down prerequisite skills that might interfere with new learning. If it's integer rules, for example, create a bookmark of those for students.

In addition to instructional strategies are attitudes about students who are struggling at school, and decisions made on their behalf. Highly self-efficacious teachers enthused about their content are often the best equipped to reignite their learning. An overreliance on courseware might not be the best fit for underperforming learners. Purposeful learning groups with real-world relevance can build content and a sense of community. Whole group instruction all day might fuel isolation.

Jumping in academically can be risky—students who are floundering are particularly sensitive to appearing clueless. But small moments of real success can be invigorating. A math problem correctly solved on a sticky note, an inspired solution with a partner, or a riveting introductory statement on an essay: these moments can bring genuine commendations.

For four years, I coordinated a program for students in a large district who had failed too many classes, failed state tests, failed something . . . It struck me that, at the school level, the numbers probably seemed small. A couple of students from this grade, more from this school, a bunch from that one. The problem at the school level probably didn't seem like an issue. The number of students retained (or socially promoted) per school felt small to them. But it adds up. And each child's school failure feeds into the community at large.

In the PD for the summer program, all of us had to first calibrate our mindsets. Rather than notice a student's cap or shirt logo or some other infraction right out of the gate, we started every morning with, "I'm so glad that you are here." We used short, humorous surveys every day to gauge how our lessons were working (including answers like "Sorry—I was catching a nap during that part"). On the final survey, many students voluntary wrote how much these teachers meant to them—how much they mattered.

These vulnerable learners may look anything but fragile. Their often-callous exteriors guard them from hurt. Do we want them in our buildings? Will we go the extra distance to change the trajectories of their lives? Will we see their strengths?

Teaching is hard work. It's particularly challenging when working with vulnerable learners. They test our resolve and resources. One book cannot provide an answer every complex issue. Across the research, however, is the unwavering truth that what educators do every day matters greatly in the lives of our children.

References

ADHD numbers: Facts, statistics, and you. (2017). Retrieved from https://www.addrc.org/adhd-numbers-facts-statistics-and-you/

Adult Literacy Facts. (2019). Retrieved from https://proliteracy.org/Adult-Literacy-Facts#

Allensworth, E., Gwynne, J. A., de la Torre, M., & Moore, P. (2014). Looking forward to high school and college middle grade indicators of readiness in Chicago public schools. Retrieved from https://consortium.uchicago.edu/publications/looking-forward-high-school-and-college-middle-grade-indicators-readiness-chicago

America's richest self-made women, *Forbes*, June 30, 2019. Page 70.

Anderson, G., Whipple, A., & Jimerson, S. (2003). Grade retention: Achievement and mental health outcomes. Center for Development and Learning. Retrieved from https://www.cdl.org/articles/grade-retention-achievement-and-mental-health-outcomes/

Archer, D. (2014, May 14). ADHD: The entrepreneur's superpower. *Forbes*. Retrieved from https://www.forbes.com/sites/dalearcher/2014/05/14/adhd-the-entrepreneurs-superpower/#55b4fc8259e9

Badenhausen, K. (2019). Serena's net gains. *Forbes*, June 20, 2019, pp. 54–60.

Baig, E. (2018, October 15). Richard Branson on dyslexics: We're wired differently. *USA Today*. Retrieved from https://www.usatoday.com/story/tech/columnist/baig/2018/10/15/richard-branson-wants-change-your-perception-people-dyslexia/1615057002/

Bailey, E., & Pransky, K. (2014). *Memory at work in the classroom: Strategies to help underachieving students*. Alexandria, VA: ASCD.

Bandura, A. (1984). Recycling misconceptions of perceived self-efficacy: *Cognitive Therapy and Research, 8*(3), 231–255.

Barbaresi, W. J., Colligan, R. C., Weaver, A. L., Voight, R. G., Killian, J. M., & Katusik, S. K. (2013). Mortality, ADHD, psychosocial adversity in adults with childhood ADHD: A prospective study. *Pediatrics, 131*(4), 637–644. doi:10.1542/peds.2012-2354

Barkley, R. A. (2017). What causes ADHD? Retrieved from http://www .russellbarkley.org/factsheets/WhatCausesADHD2017.pdf

Barshaw, J. (2019). Gifted classes may not help talented students move ahead faster. The Hechinger Report. Retrieved from https://hechingerreport .org/gifted-classes-may-not-help-talented-students-move-ahead-faster/

Betts, G. T., & Neihart, M. (1988). Profiles of the gifted and talented. *Gifted Child Quarterly, 32*(2), 248–253. Retrieved from http://maryschmidt .pbworks.com/f/Gifted%2520Child%2520Quarterly-1988-Betts-248 -53.pdf

Biederman, J., Petty, C. R., Clarke, A., Lomedico, A., & Faraone, S. V. (2011). Predictors of persistent ADHD: An 11-year follow-up study. *Journal of Psychiatric Research, 45*(2), 150–155. doi:10.1016/j.jpsychires.2010.06.009

Black, P., & William, D. (1998). Inside the black box: Raising standards through classroom assessment. *Phi Delta Kappan, 80*(2), 139–148.

Blass, S. (2014). The relationship between social-emotional difficulties and underachievement of gifted students. *Australian Journal of Guidance and Counseling, 24*(2), 243–255. Retrieved from https://cpb-us-e1.wpmucdn .com/cobblearning.net/dist/0/2262/files/2016/04/The-Relationship -Between-Social-Emotional-Dificulties-and-Underachievement-of-Gifted -Students-1p7wok6.pdf

Boccanfuso, C. & Kuhfield, M. (2011). Multiple responses promising results: evidence-based, nonpunitive alternatives to zero tolerance. *Child Trends Research to Results Brief,* 2011-09. Retrieved from http://www.nea.org /assets/docs/alternatives-to-zero-tolerance.pdf

Brasch, B. (2018, September 19). Graduation rates increased for most Cobb high schools in 2018. *Atlanta Journal-Constitution.* Retrieved from https://www.ajc.com/news/local/graduation-rates-increased-for-most -cobb-high-schools-2018/8BFvulRxfbne3kN0ZmxOGI/

Bridgeland, J. M., DiIulio, J. J., & Morison, K. B. (2006). The silent epidemic:

Perspectives of high school dropouts. Gates Foundation. Retrieved from https://docs.gatesfoundation.org/documents/thesilentepidemic3 -06final.pdf

Brooks, K., Adams, S. R., & Morita-Mullaney, T. (2010). Creating inclusive learning communities for ELL students: Transforming school principals' perspectives. Retrieved from https://digitalcommons.butler.edu /cgi/viewcontent.cgi?article=1001&context=coe_papers

Brophy, J. (2010). *Motivating students to learn*. New York: Routledge.

Bruner, M. S. (1993). Reduced recidivism and increased employment opportunity through research-based reading instruction. Department of Justice, Washington, DC, ED 361 646. Retrieved from https://files .eric.ed.gov/fulltext/ED361646.pdf

Burke, A. (2015). Early identification of high school graduation outcomes. Institute of Education Sciences. Retrieved from https://ies.ed.gov/ncee /edlabs/regions/northwest/pdf/REL_2015079.pdf

Callahan, R., Wilkinson, L., & Muller, C. (2010). Academic achievement and course taking among language minority youth in U.S. schools: Effects of ESL placement. *Educational Evaluation and Policy Analysis*, 32(1), 84–117. doi:10.3102/0162373709359805

Carnevale, A. P., Smith, N., & Strohl, J. (2014). Recovery: Job growth and education requirements. Retrieved from https://1gyhoq479ufd3yna29x7ubjn -wpengine.netdna-ssl.com/wp-content/uploads/2014/11/Recovery2020 .ES_.Web_.pdf

Carr, S. (2017, May 24). Online education doesn't have to be isolating. *Slate*. Retrieved from https://slate.com/news-and-politics/2017/05/bronx-arena -is-doing-online-credit-recovery-right.html

Centers for Disease Control. (n.d.). Symptoms and diagnosis of ADHD. Retrieved from https://www.cdc.gov/ncbddd/adhd/diagnosis.html

Chapman, C., Laird, J., Ifill, N., & KewalRamani, A. (2011). Trends in high school dropout and completion rates: 1972–2009. U.S. Department of Education, National Center for Education Statistics. Retrieved from https://nces.ed.gov/pubs2012/2012006.pdf

Colangelo, N., Assouline, S. G., & Cross, M. (2004). A nation deceived: How schools hold back America's brightest students. Retrieved from https:// files.eric.ed.gov/fulltext/ED535137.pdf

Consequences of Illiteracy. (2019). Literacy Foundation. Retrieved from https://www.fondationalphabetisation.org/en/causes-of-illiteracy/consequences-of-illiteracy/

Couloute, L., & Kopf, D. (2018). Out of prison and out of work: Unemployment among formerly incarcerated people. Prison Policy Initiative. Retrieved from https://www.prisonpolicy.org/reports/outofwork.html

Cross, T. L. (2018). *On the social and emotional lives of gifted children*. Waco, TX: Prufrock Press.

Cross, T. L., Andersen, L., & Maddadov, S. (2015). Effects of academic acceleration on the social and emotional lives of gifted students. In S. Assouline, N. Colangelo, J. Van Tassel-Baska, & A. Lupkowski-Shoplik (Eds.), *A nation empowered*, 31–42. Retrieved from https://www.shorelineschools.org/cms/lib/WA02217114/Centricity/Domain/90/NationEmpowered_Vol2.pdf

Davidson Institute. (2019). Support for gifted programs vary greatly from state to state. Retrieved from https://www.davidsongifted.org/Search-Database/entryType/3

Denton, K., & West, J. (2002). Children's reading and mathematics achievement in kindergarten and first grade. US Department of Education, National Center for Educational Statistics. Retrieved from https://nces.ed.gov/pubs2002/2002125.pdf

Doll, J. J., Eslami, Z., & Walters, L. (2013, October). Understanding why students drop out of high school, according to their own reports: Are they pushed or pulled, or do they fall out? A comparative analysis of seven nationally represented studies. *SAGE Open*, 1–15. Retrieved from https://journals.sagepub.com/doi/pdf/10.1177/2158244013503834

Dopfel, K., Biden, A., & Kuprevich, C. (2013). Criminal justice and ADHD: There are solutions. Washington, DC: National Association of Case Management.

Doyle, A. (2019). The best ADHD apps for 2019. Retrieved from https://www.healthline.com/health/adhd/top-iphone-android-apps

Dynarski, S. (2018, January 19). Online courses are harming the students who need the most help. *New York Times*. Retrieved from https://www.nytimes.com/2018/01/19/business/online-courses-are-harming-the-students-who-need-the-most-help.html

Dyslexia Help. (2019). Success and Inspirational Stories: Stephen J. Cannell. Retrieved from http://dyslexiahelp.umich.edu/success-stories/stephen-cannell

Editors of ADDitude. (2015). Great sports and activities for kids with ADHD. Retrieved from https://www.additudemag.com/wp-content/uploads/2017/01/10227_For-Parents_great-sports-and-activities-for-kids-with-adhd.pdf

Education Commission of the States. (2016). State policies—third grade retention. Retrieved from https://www.ecs.org/wp-content/uploads/SIR-Retention.pdf

ElDaou, B., & El-Shamieh, S. (2014). The effect of playing chess on the concentration of ADHD student in the 2nd cycle. *Procedia: Social and Behavioral Sciences, 192,* 638–643. Retrieved from https://www.sciencedirect.com/science/article/pii/S187704281503582X

Erben, T., Ban, R., & Castaneda, M. (2009). *Teaching English language learners through technology.* New York: Routledge.

Felitti, V.J., Anda, R.F., Nordenberg, D., Williamson, D.F., Spitz, A.M., Edwards, V., . . . Marks, J.S. (1998). Relationship of childhood abuse and household dysfunction to many of the leading causes of death in adults. America Journal of Preventive Medicine. Retrieved from https://www.ncbi.nlm.nih.gov/pubmed/9635069

Fenner, D. S., & Snyder, S. (2017). *Unlocking English learners' potential: Strategies for making content accessible.* Thousand Oaks, CA: Corwin.

Ferlazzo, L., & Sypnieski, K. H. (2018). *The ELL teacher's toolbox: Hundreds of practical ideas to support your students.* San Francisco: Jossey-Bass.

Fletcher, J., & Wolfe, B. (2009). Long-term consequences of childhood ADHD on criminal activities. *Journal of Mental Health Policy and Economics, 12*(3), 119–138.

Flippen, R. (2020). Hyperfocus: The ADHD phenomenon of intense fixation. Retrieved from: https://www.additudemag.com/understanding-adhd-hyperfocus/

Freudenberg, N., & Ruglis, J. (2007). Reframing school dropout as a public health issue. *Preventing Chronic Disease, 4*(4), A107.

Frye, D. (2017, spring). Children left behind. *ADDitude Magazine.* Retrieved from https://www.additudemag.com/race-and-adhd-how-people-of-color-get-left-behind/

Galuschka, K., & Schulte-Körne, G. (2016). The diagnosis and treatment of reading and/or spelling disorders in children and adolescents. *Deutsches Arzteblatt International, 113*(16), 279–286. doi:10.3238/arztebl.2016.0279

Gibbs, A. (2017). How Richard Branson's mother turned the entrepreneur into an adventurer from a very early age. Retrieved from: https://www.cnbc.com/2017/11/14/richard-branson-and-his-adventurous-entrepreneurial-spirit.html

Glader, S. (2019). Daymond John, Entrepreneur. Yale Center for Dyslexia and Creativity. Retrieved from https://dyslexia.yale.edu/story/daymond-john/

Gladwell, M. (2013). *David and Goliath: Underdogs, misfits and the art of battling giants*. Boston: Little, Brown.

Gonzales, T. (2012). Keeping kids in schools: Restorative justice punitive discipline, and the school to prison pipeline. *Journal of Law and Education, 41*(2), 281–335. Retrieved from http://www.ibarji.org/docs/gonzales.pdf

Green, A. L., & Rabiner, D. L. (2012). What do we really know about ADHD in college students? *Neurotherapeutics, 9*(3), 559–568. doi:10.1007/s13311-012-0127-8

Grohol, J. M. (2019). Famous people with ADHD. Retrieved from: https://psychcentral.com/lib/famous-people-with-adhd/

Guthrie, J. T., Wigfield, A., Barbosa, P., Perencevich, K. C., Taboada, A., Davis, M. H., Scafiddi, N. T., & Tonks, S. (2004). Increasing reading comprehension and engagement through concept-oriented reading instruction. *Journal of Educational Psychology, 96*(3), 403–423. Retrieved from http://www.cori.umd.edu/research-publications/2004-guthrie-wigfield-etal.pdf

Hallowell, E. (n.d.). Your brain is a Ferrari. Retrieved from https://www.additudemag.com/how-to-explain-adhd-to-a-child-and-build-confidence/

Hallowell, E., & Ratey, J. (2011). *Driven to distraction*. New York: Anchor.

Hanover Research. (2017). Best practices for grade 9 transitions. Retrieved from https://www.wasa-oly.org/WASA/images/WASA/1.0%20Who%20We%20Are/1.4.1.6%20SIRS/Download_Files/LI%202018/Jan-Best%20Practices%20for%20Grade%209%20Transitions.pdf

Harlen, W., & Crick, R. (2003). Testing and motivation for learning. *Assessment in Education, 10*(2), 169–207.

Hansen, D. (1989). Lesson evading and lesson dissembling: Ego strategies in the classroom. *American Journal of Education, 97*(2), 184–208.

Hart, B., & Risley, T. R. (1995). *Meaningful differences in the everyday experiences of young American children*. Baltimore, MD: Paul H. Brookes.

Hattie, J. & Yates, G. (2014). *Visible learning and the science of how we learn*. New York: Routledge.

Hiefield, M. (2018). How we empowered and engaged Latino parents— by building a tech community. EdSurge. Retrieved from https://www .edsurge.com/news/2018-03-02-how-we-empowered-and-engaged-latino -parents-by-building-a-tech-community

Hoagies' Gifted Education Page. (n.d.). Gifted education mandates, by state or province. Retrieved from https://www.hoagiesgifted.org/mandates .htm#usa

Hoy, A. & Davis, H. (2006). Teacher self-efficacy and its influence on the achievement of adolescents. In F. Pajares & T. Urdan (Eds.), *Self-efficacy beliefs of adolescents* (pp. 117–137). Greenwich, CT: Information Age Publishing.

Holland, K., & Riley, E. (2017). ADHD numbers: Facts, statistics, and you. Retrieved from https://www.addrc.org/adhd-numbers-facts-statistics -and-you/

Hurley, P. J., & Eme, R. (2004). *ADHD and the criminal justice system: Spinning out of control*. Abstract retrieved from https://www.ncjrs.gov/App /Publications/abstract.aspx?ID=208348

Jarrett, C. (2018, May 1). How prison changes people. BBC Future. Retrieved from http://www.bbc.com/future/story/20180430-the-unexpected-ways -prison-time-changes-people

Jasper, K. (2016). The effects of third grade retention on standard diploma acquisition and student outcomes: A policy analysis of Florida's A+ plan (Doctoral dissertation). Florida Gulf Coast University. Retrieved from https://static1.squarespace.com/static/55e6f66ae4b084d88962a8c7/t /5879fbe7db29d69a1a1986d0/1484389353620/Jasper-Final_Dissertation -ProQuest.pdf

Jennings, P.A. (2019). *Trauma-sensitive classroom: Building resilience with compassionate teaching*. New York: W.W. Norton.

Jensen, L. (2006). New immigrant settlements in rural America: Problems, prospects, and policies. Carsey Institute, University of New Hampshire. Retrieved from https://scholars.unh.edu/cgi/viewcontent.cgi?article =1016&context=carsey

Jimerson, S. (2001). Meta-analysis of grade retention research: Implications for practice in the 21st century. *School Psychology Review, 30*(3), 420–437.

Jimerson, S., & Renshaw, T. (2012, September). Retention and social promotion. *Principal Leadership.*

Jordan, W. J., Lara, J., & McPartland, J. M. (1994). *Exploring the complexity of early dropout causal structures.* Baltimore, MD: Center for Research on Effective Schooling for Disadvantaged Students, Johns Hopkins University.

Joszt, L. (2017, November 29). Brain MRI's can identify ADHD and distinguish among subtypes. *AJMC.* Retrieved from https://www.ajmc.com/newsroom/brain-mris-can-identify-adhd-and-distinguish-among-subtypes

Kalb, G., & van Ours, J. (2013). Reading to younger children: A head-start in life? Institute for the Study of Labor, no. 7416. Retrieved from http://ftp.iza.org/dp7416.pdf

Kanno, Y., & Cromley, J. (2015). English language learners' pathways to four-year colleges. *Teachers College Record, 117*(120306). Retrieved from http://www.bu.edu/wheelock/files/2016/10/Kanno-Cromley-2015.pdf

Kaplan, L. S. (1990). Helping gifted students with stress management. Retrieved from http://www.casenex.com/casenex/ericReadings/HelpingGiftedStudents.pdf

Kaufmann, F., Kalbfleisch, M. L., & Castellanos, F. X. (2000). Attention deficit disorders and gifted students: What do we really know? National Research Center on the Gifted and Talented. Retrieved from https://nrcgt.uconn.edu/wp-content/uploads/sites/953/2015/04/rm00146.pdf

Kerr, S. P., Kerr, W. R., & Xu, T. (2017). Personality traits of entrepreneurs: A review of recent literature. Harvard Business School, Working Paper 18-047. Retrieved from https://www.hbs.edu/faculty/Publication%20Files/18-047_b0074a64-5428-479b-8c83-16f2a0e97eb6.pdf

Kids Count Data Center. (2018, January). The number of bilingual kids in America continues to rise. Retrieved from https://datacenter.kidscount.org/updates/show/184-the-number-of-bilingual-kids-in-america-continues-to-rise

Kirkpatrick, D. A. (2015). *Essentials of assessing, preventing, and overcoming reading difficulties.* Hoboken, NJ: John Wiley & Sons.

Kuriyan, A. B., Pelham, W. E., Jr, Molina, B. S., Waschbusch, D. A., Gnagy, E. M., Sibley, M. H., . . . Kent, K. M. (2013). Young adult educational and vocational outcomes of children diagnosed with ADHD. *Journal of Abnormal Child Psychology, 41*(1), 27–41. doi:10.1007/s10802-012-9658-z

Langrehr, J. (2019, July 3). Creative, curious, and challenging thinking. *Teacher.* Retrieved from https://www.teachermagazine.com.au/articles/creative-curious-and-challenging-thinking

Literacy Foundation. (2019). Consequences of illiteracy. Retrieved from https://www.fondationalphabetisation.org/en/causes-of-illiteracy/consequences-of-illiteracy/

Lumsden, L. S. (1994). Student motivation to learn. *ERIC Digest,* no. 92. Retrieved from https://files.eric.ed.gov/fulltext/ED370200.pdf

Mahoney, J. L., & Cairns, R. B. (1997). Do extracurricular activities protect against early school dropout? *Developmental Psychology, 33*(2), 241–253. Retrieved from https://static1.squarespace.com/static/5951da046a4963bbc7c45f50/t/5a61b2d471c10ba72c775a71/1516352213967/%28Mahoney+%26+Cairns+19

Marzano, R. I. (2004). *Building background knowledge for academic achievement: Research on what works in schools.* Alexandria, VA: ASCD.

Mather, N. & Wendling, B.J. (2012). *Essentials of dyslexia assessment and intervention.* Hoboken, NJ: John Wiley & Sons.

Moody, K. C., Holzer, C. E., Roman, M. J., Paulson, K. A., Freeman, D. H., Haynes, M., & James, T. N. (2000). Prevalence of dyslexia among Texas inmates. *Texas Medicine, 96*(6), 69–75. Retrieved from https://www.ncbi.nlm.nih.gov/pubmed/10876375

Morgan, P. L., Farkas, G., Tufis, P., & Sperling, R. (2008). Are reading and behavior problems risk factors for each other? *Journal of Learning Disabilities, 41*(5), 417–436. Retrieved from https://www.ncbi.nlm.nih.gov/pmc/articles/PMC4422059/

Morgan, P. L., Farkas, G., & Wu, Q. (2012). Do poor readers feel angry, sad, unpopular? *Scientific Studies of Reading, 16*(4), 360–381. doi:10.1080/10888438.2011.570397

Morton, I. (1992). Increasing the school involvement of Hispanic parents. *ERIC/CUE Digest,* no. 80. Retrieved from https://www.ericdigests.org/1992-1/hispanic.htm

Moughamian, A. C., Rivera, M. O., & Francis, D. J. (2009). Instructional models and strategies for teaching English language learners. Portsmouth, NH: RMC Research Corporation, Center on Instruction. Retrieved from https://files.eric.ed.gov/fulltext/ED517794.pdf

Murphey, D. (2014). The academic achievement of English language learners. *Child Trends*, 2014-62. Retrieved from https://www.childtrends.org/wp-content/uploads/2015/07/2014-62AcademicAchievementEnglish.pdf

NAEP. (2017). NAEP mathematics and reading assessments. National Assessment of Educational Progress. Retrieved from https://www.nationsreportcard.gov/reading_math_2017_highlights/

Nagy, W. E., & Townsend, D. (2012). Words as tools: Learning academic vocabulary as language acquisition. *Reading Research Quarterly, 47*(1), 91–108.

National Center for Education. (2012). Schools and staffing survey. Retrieved from https://nces.ed.gov/surveys/sass/tables/sass1112_498_t1n.asp

National Center for Education Statistics. (2019, May). English language learners in public schools. Retrieved from https://nces.ed.gov/programs/coe/indicator_cgf.asp

National Reading Panel. (2000). *Teaching children to read: An evidence-based assessment of the scientific research literature on reading and its implications for reading instruction*. NIH Publication No. 00-04754. Retrieved from https://www.nichd.nih.gov/sites/default/files/publications/pubs/nrp/Documents/report.pdf

Neihart, M., Pfeiffer, S. I., & Cross, T. L. (2016). *The social and emotional development of gifted children*. Waco, TX: Prufrock.

Office for Civil Rights. (2012). 2011–12 state and national estimations. Retrieved from https://ocrdata.ed.gov/StateNationalEstimations/Estimations_2011_12

Oppedisano, A., & Goffredo, A. (2017). Acceleration: Moving students in the right direction. *Apprendre et Enseigner Aujourd'hui, 7*(1), 37–43. Retrieved from https://fr.calameo.com/read/001898804de933eb6e8e4

Pajares, F. (2006). Self-efficacy during childhood and adolescence: Implications for teachers and parents. In F. Pajares & T. Urdan (Eds.), *Self-efficacy beliefs of adolescents* (pp. 339-367). Greenwich, CT: Information Age Publishing.

Parental involvement in schools. (2013). *Child Trends*. Retrieved from https://www.childtrends.org/?indicators=parental-involvement-in-schools

Petersen, R. (2005). Ten alternatives to suspension. *Impact, 18*(2) 10–11. Retrieved from https://ici.umn.edu/products/impact/182/182.pdf

Plucker, J. A., & Callahan, C. M. (2014). Research on giftedness and gifted education: Status of the field and considerations for the future. *Exceptional Children, 80*(4), 390–406. doi:10.1177/0014402914527244

Powell, C. (1980). A meta-analysis of the effects of "imposed" and "induced" imagery upon word recall. Retrieved from https://files.eric.ed.gov/fulltext/ED199644.pdf

Quintero, D., & Hansen, M. (2017). English learners and the growing need for qualified teachers. Retrieved from https://www.brookings .edu/blog/brown-center-chalkboard/2017/06/02/english-learners-and -the-growing-need-for-qualified-teachers/

Quiocho, A. M. I., & Daoud, A. M. (2006). Dispelling myths about Latino parent participation in schools. *Educational Forum, 70,* 255–267. Retrieved from https://files.eric.ed.gov/fulltext/EJ735839.pdf

Renzulli, J. S., & Park, S. (2002). Giftedness and high school dropouts: Personal, family, and school-related factors. National Research Center on the Gifted and Talented. Retrieved from https://files.eric.ed.gov/ fulltext/ED480177.pdf

Robertson, E. (1991). Neglected dropouts: The gifted and talented. *Equity and Excellence, 25*(1), 62–73. https://doi.org/10.1080/1066568910250112

Robertson, K., & Ford, K. (n.d.). Language acquisition: An overview. Colorín Colorado! Retrieved from https://www.colorincolorado.org/article /language-acquisition-overview

Rodriquez, A. (2017, August 24). Gender differences in the brain explain why men have higher rates of ADHD. *AJMC.* Retrieved from https:// www.ajmc.com/newsroom/gender-differences-in-the-brain-explain -why-men-have-higher-rates-of-adhd

Rollins, S. P. (2014). Learning in the fast lane: 8 ways to put all students on the road to success. Alexandria, VA: ASCD.

Ruggiero, M. J. (2012). Effects of gifted and talented programs on standardized test scores on fourth grade students in two school districts (master's thesis). State University of New York at Fredonia. Retrieved from https://dspace.sunyconnect.suny.edu/bitstream/handle/1951/58356 /Melinda_Ruggiero_Masters_Project_May2012.pdf

Sanchez, C. (2017). English language learners: How your state is doing. NPR.

Retrieved from https://www.npr.org/sections/ed/2017/02/23/512451228/5 -million-english-language-learners-a-vast-pool-of-talent-at-risk

School dropouts and their impact on the criminal justice system. (2012). Task Force to Study High School Dropout Rates of Persons in the Criminal Justice System. Retrieved from http://dlslibrary.state.md.us/ publications/Exec/GOCCP/SB755Ch286_2011.pdf

Schuler, P. A. (2000). Perfectionism and gifted adolescents. *Journal of Secondary Gifted Education, 11*(4), 183–196. Retrieved from https://citeseerx.ist.psu.edu/viewdoc/download?doi=10.1.1.893 .824&rep=repl&type=pdf

Schunk, D.H. & Meese, J.L. (2006). Self-efficacy development in adolescence. In F. Pajares & T. Urdan (Eds.), Self-efficacy beliefs of adolescents (pp. 71–96). Greenwich, CT: Information Age Publishing.

Shankman, P. (Producer). (2017). Using ADHD to start an airline, with Jetblue founder David Neeleman. *Faster Than Normal*, no. 66. Retrieved from https://www.fasterthannormal.com/ftn-66-using-adhd-to-start-an -airline-with-jetblue-founder-david-neeleman/

Shaywitz, S. (2003). *Overcoming dyslexia: A new and complete science-based program for reading problems at any level.* New York: Vintage.

Shearer, B., Ruddell, M., & Vogt, M. (2001). Successful middle school reading intervention: Negotiated strategies and individual choice. *National Reading Conference Yearbook, 50*, 558–571.

Sousa, D. A., & Tomlinson, C. A. (2011). *Differentiation and the brain: How neuroscience supports the learner-friendly classroom.* Bloomington, IN: Solution Tree Press.

Southern, W. T., & Jones, E. D. (2015). Types of acceleration: Dimensions and issues. In S. Assouline, N. Colangelo, J. Van Tassel-Baska, & A. Lupkowski-Shoplik (Eds.), *A nation empowered*, 9–18. Retrieved from https://www.shorelineschools.org/cms/lib/WA02217114/Centricity/ Domain/90/NationEmpowered_Vol2.pdf

Stahl, S. A., & Fairbanks, M. M. (1986). The effects of vocabulary instruction: A model-based meta-analysis. *Review of Educational Research, 56*(1), 72–110.

Stanovich, K.E. (1986). Matthew effects in reading: Some consequences of individual differences in the acquisition of literacy. *Reading Research Quarterly, 21*(4), 360–406.

Stark, L. (2019, April 30). What parents of dyslexic children are teaching schools about literacy. *PBS Newshour*. Retrieved from https://www.pbs.org/newshour/show/what-parents-of-dyslexic-children-are-teaching-schools-about-literacy

Stark, P., Noel, A. M., & McFarland, J. (2015). Trends in high school dropout and completion rates: 1972–2012. U.S. Department of Education, National Center for Education Statistics. Retrieved from https://nces.ed.gov/pubs2015/2015015.pdf

Steele, J. L., Slater, R., Zamarro, G., Miller, T., Li, J. J., Burkhauser, S., & Bacon, M. (2017). Dual-language immersion programs raise student achievement in English. RAND Corporation. Retrieved from https://www.rand.org/pubs/research_briefs/RB9903.html

Stevens, J. (2012). Lincoln high school in Walla Walla, WA tries new approach to school discipline – suspensions down 85%. *Aces Too High News*. Retrieved from https://acestoohigh.com/2012/04/23/lincoln-high-school-in-walla-walla-wa-tries-new-approach-to-school-discipline-expulsions-drop-85/

Stuit, D., O'Cummings, M., Norbury, H., Heppen, J., Dhillon, S., Lindsay, J., & Zhu, B. (2016). Identifying early warning indicators in three Ohio school districts. Institute of Education Sciences. Retrieved from https://ies.ed.gov/ncee/edlabs/regions/midwest/pdf/REL_2016118.pdf

Sun, H., Chen, Y., Huang, Q., Lui, S. Huang, X., Shi, Y., Xu, X., Sweeney, J., & Gong, Q. (2017). Psychoradiologic utility of MR imaging for diagnosis of attention deficit hyperactivity disorder: A radiomics analysis. *Radiology, 287*(2). https://doi.org/10.1148/radiol.2017170226

Tambornino, R. (2019). From canned to competencies: Why we canned the "canned" curriculum. *Engage*. Retrieved from: http://www.dropoutprevention.org/engage-backup/from-computers-to-competencies-why-we-canned-the-canned-curriculum/

U.S. Department of Education, National Center for Education Statistics (2011). Trends in high school dropout and completion rates: 1972-2009. Retrieved from: https://nces.ed.gov/pubs2012/2012006.pdf

U.S. Department of Education, National Center for Education Statistics (2015). Trends in high school dropout and completion rates: 1972-2012. Retrieved from: https://nces.ed.gov/pubs2015/2015015.pdf

U.S. Department of Education. (2016). Issue brief: Early warning systems.

Retrieved from https://www2.ed.gov/rschstat/eval/high-school/early-warning-systems-brief.pdf

U.S. Department of Education. (2019). School climate and discipline: Know the data. Retrieved from https://www2.ed.gov/policy/gen/guid/school-discipline/data.html

U.S. Department of Education (n.d.). Our nation's English learners. Retrieved from https://www2.ed.gov/datastory/el-characteristics/index.html#intro

Usher, E. & Pajares, F. (2008). Sources of self-efficacy in school: Critical review of the literature and future directions. *Review of Educational Research*, 78(4), 751-796.

Van Der Kolk, B. (2014). *The body keeps the score: Brain, mind, and body in the healing of trauma*. New York: Penguin Books.

VanTassel-Baska, J. (2005). Gifted programs and services: What are the nonnegotiables? *Theory into Practice, 44*(2), 90–97. Retrieved from https://www.franklinschools.org/cms/lib/IN01001624/Centricity/Domain/31/VanTassel-Baska%20-%202005%20-%20Gifted%20Programs%20and%20Services%20What%20Are%20the%20Nonnego.pdf

Watt, D., & Roessingh, H. (1994). Some you win, most you lose: Tracking ESL dropout in high school (1988–1993). *English Quarterly, 26*, 5–7.

Webb, J., Gore, J., Amend, E., & DeVries, A. (2007). *A parent's guide to gifted children.* Tucson, AZ: Great Potential.

Willis, J. (2006). *Research-based strategies to ignite student learning: Insights from a neurologist and classroom teacher.* Alexandria, VA: ASCD

Young, S., Gudjonsson, G., Chitsabesan, P., Colley, B., Farrag, E., Forrester, A., . . . Asherson, P. (2018). Identification and treatment of offenders with attention-deficit/hyperactivity disorder in the prison population: A practical approach based upon expert consensus. *BMC Psychiatry, 18*(1), 281. doi:10.1186/s12888-018-1858-9

Zimmerman, B.J. & Cleary, T.J. (2006). Adolescents' development of personal agency. In F. Pajares & T.Urdan (Eds.) S*elf-efficacy beliefs of adolescents* (pp. 45–69). Greenwich, CT: Information Age Publishing.

Index

Note: Italicized page locators refer to figures.

About the Author

Suzy Pepper Rollins is a passionate, high-energy educator with a mission of creating academic success in all learners. Author of Learning in the Fast Lane and Teaching in the Fast Lane, both published by ASCD, she is also the founder of Math in the Fast Lane, a hands-on approach to teaching math (www.mathinfastlane.com). She consults with districts across the nation and beyond and prides herself on professional development that yields next-day implementation. Her newest project is www.MyEdExpert.com, an online space in which authors share their resources with the larger ed community. The best way to reach Suzy is through her website, www.SuzyPepperRollins.com or on Twitter @myedexpert.